Negotiating Intimacies

NEGOTIATING INTIMACIES

Sexualities, Birth Control and Poor Households

Arna Seal

Stree

NEGOTIATING INTIMACIES
Sexualities, Birth Control and Poor Households
was first published in January 2000 by Stree
16 Southern Avenue, Calcutta 700 026

ISBN 81-85604-29-0

Distributed by Popular Prakashan Pvt Ltd
Mumbai, Calcutta, Delhi

Typesetting and design by
LOGS, 6 Ram Hari Mistry Lane, Calcutta 700 013
and printed by Webimpressions (India) Pvt Ltd
34/2 Beadon St, Calcutta 700 006

Published by Mandira Sen for STREE, an imprint of
Bhatkal and Sen, 16 Southern Ave, Cacutta 700 026

To Ma, Bapi and Rima : My first family

ACKNOWLEDGEMENTS

Writing this book has been like embarking on a long journey that has just come to an end. I began the research as a postgraduate in the Sociology Department of Tulane University at New Orleans, and wrote the book after I returned to Calcutta. It seemed to be a complicated, long-drawn effort, and at times it felt as if the journey would never come to an end. I owe many people a debt of gratitude. I do believe that without their help I would not have succeeded in completing the research or the book. I would like to thank Professor Marlena M. Studer, my Ph.D. advisor, guide and friend who gave freely of her time and helped me to finalize the conceptual framework of the study. I am grateful to Professor Joseph F. Sheley who encouraged me to carry on with qualitative primary research at a time when most postgraduates were focused on quantitative outputs with large-scale secondary data sets. Professor J. Timmons Roberts (Tim) introduced me to the pathbreaking work of Lourdes Beneria and Martha Roldan (*The Crossroads of Class and Gender: Industrial Homework, Subcontracting and Household Dynamics in Mexico City*) that has been a major inspiration on my research, helping me to perceive what happens locally in a global context.

I benefited enormously from the help, warmth and friendship I received from fellow students without which I would not have been able to live happily in the United States or even complete my research. I think with appreciation and nostalgia of Danilo Levi (who is now in the Honduras) for our long conversations on globalization and pauperization over those many student lunches that we ate together. Bryan Langs typed up all my tables, formatted and printed out my thesis and brought in groceries when I was frantically writing to meet my deadlines. Jane Kuroda taught me WordPerfect, made my photocopies and stuffed me with her delicious cream puffs whenever she felt that my glucose level was falling. Dear friends like Gunja Sengupta and Sunita and Sabita Manian always made me feel proud of this work. They added zest to my life, providing the 'breaks' in town, the weekends spent at the French Quarter, whenever I needed to distance myself from my research. I thank Priyodarshi Majumdar for being the typical

Bengali 'bhai', cooking simple and delicious lunches when I had no time to cook. I owe a special debt to Salim Darbar for his constant support and reticent care which enabled me to complete my work successfully.

I gratefully acknowledge the help of Ajit Pati of the Ramakrishna Lok Shiksha Parishad who helped with the preparation of the questionnaire and enabled me to gain access to the women in the slums. I would like to thank Rita Dey, my partner at Development Management Consultants, for her support, and the other colleagues, especially Uma Mahato, Shyamal Ghosh, Tathagata Roy and Neela Dhori for their help with typing and updating references. Without the assistance of Anita Sinai Basu and Swati Sengupta who helped me with rearranging chapters, editing and updating the references, the book would never have been completed. I am also appreciative of the support of Moushumi Bhowmik, Rimi Chatterjee and Mandira Sen of Stree who insisted that I could complete the book despite the rival demands of career, marriage and motherhood.

I have been very fortunate in the support and encouragement that I have received from my family. My mother, Sucharita Seal, and my mother-in-law, Kana Acharya, shared my household and baby-sitting responsibilities at a time when I often felt overwhelmed by domestic commitments. My father, Utpal Seal, and sister, Aeshna, remained consistently encouraging. I don't have words to thank my husband, Srikanto Acharya, who collected all the official data I needed at the research stage and who remained patient and forbearing throughout the long gestation of this book. And finally I would like to say something about my three-and-a-half-year-old daughter, Proiti, who with her wide-eyed expectations has taught me to see the women's lives I have written about through the mother's eye, enabling me in the process to feel a deeper sense of bonding with them.

CONTENTS

Introduction

After the usual repertory of family anecdotes, mother's letter went on:

> 'Annapurna had a tubectomy last month. Her husband does not know. If he knew, he wouldn't have allowed it. There were three or four other women in her slum who wanted to undergo sterilization. So they went to a local hospital and got themselves operated upon. She took leave from us and her other three employers but she hardly got any rest because, as usual, she had to do all the housework in her house, with some help from her sisters. She told me that she could not lie down to rest because her husband would start to suspect .'

I put down the letter. It was a winter afternoon in New Orleans some years ago. I had not seen Annapurna for some time. She had been working as a part-time domestic servant in our house in Calcutta for the last six years. Her duties included doing our dishes twice a day and making our afternoon tea. I remembered her thin, too thin, frame. Her dark chiselled face. Eyes that barely looked up. Her oiled hair was always tied up in a knot with a line of bright red vermilion, a symbol of the sanctity of her marriage, running across the length of her forehead. The brightness of the vermilion stood in sharp contrast to the faded blue and green saris she wore to work on alternate days. When asked what she did with the other saris she received yearly from her employers, she would say she was saving them for the right occasion. I suppose her right occasions never came because I never did see her wearing them. Annapurna's starched and ironed saris stayed tucked away somewhere in a tin trunk in the bamboo loft of her tiny room, the only one making up her house. Meanwhile, she worked in four houses: doing dishes, washing clothes, mopping the floor, from six in the morning till eight in the evening with only an afternoon break for lunch and for her own housework.

Annapurna was always busy. Often in the late evenings I would see her rushing to the bazar to shop for food and provisions for the following day or to bring her children from the tutor's. Annapurna had three children. Her husband did not work. He used to work as a carpenter once but had been laid off from a permanent job and 'did not like' taking up temporary piecemeal work. This, of course, did not deter him from taking on a second wife. He shuttled between the two households while his wives worked desperately to make ends meet and to bear him children. And when Annapurna wanted to stop having children she, naturally, could not tell her husband to take any birth control measures.

We knew of Annapurna's story from her sister, who told us of the husband's second wife, his alcoholism and his regular beatings. On the days her husband beat her, Annapurna would come with swollen cheeks and bruised eyes, quietly ask my father for some painkillers, do her work and leave. Her gender subordination was so intense that in spite of the fact that she supported her family virtually alone (with some help from her matrilineal kin), she would get offended if we as much as breathed a word against her husband.

There are hundreds of thousands of Annapurnas perched on one of the most precarious edges of human existence. They come from poor agricultural families, live in urban subproletarian households, and work in the informal sector in one of the lowest paying occupations. Following eighteen-hour work days, they must endure sexual encounters with inebriated husbands, responsibilities as mothers of little children, duties as daughters-in-law and a hundred other concerns integral to the daily survival of poor working class women eking out an existence in the Third World.

Annapurna's tubectomy or, more precisely, the manner in which she achieved it, was, in my view, a manifestation of the power struggles within her household. It reflected her effort to carve out a space within the class and gender limits of her daily existence. Due to the particular nature of the power dynamics in her household, Annapurna could not tell her husband about the operation. What was the nature of bargaining and negotiation that took place between Annapurna and her husband on their mutual sexual relations? How was the issue of birth control tackled between the two? In a larger context, why, how, under what conditions and with what consequences do women, in this case slum dwellers living in an Indian metropolis, pursue the birth control careers they do? More concretely, what is the nature of gender articulation and material resource allocation and control in the household within which poor women in the Third World carve out their sexual and birth control histories? What consequences do these processes have in terms of changing and/or re-enforcing women's gender and class positions?

I chose to study this process in the context of urban working class women. The issue of birth control is often viewed as a raging 'problem' in rural India. But does it always make sense to dichotomize problems of the rural and urban in terms of residence? Most demographic studies are also geared along these lines, ignoring in the process (as Dyson and Crook [1984] pointed out) class differences within the urban and rural populations. Also, continuous focus on rural 'population problems' and the low birth rate in urban regions vis-à-vis rural India often undermines the fact that urban slum and pavement dwellers and the most marginalized socioeconomic classes in urban India tend to have fertility rates comparable to the high fertility groups in the villages (Michaelson 1981; Lebra et al. 1984; Basu 1992).

Moreover, within a particular region (urban or rural) social class may affect differentially the life chances of different groups of women in terms of access to contraception, income, and so on. And since urban crowding and urban poverty in India, specifically in Calcutta, have generated some of the most 'brutal and inhuman living conditions' on earth (The Indian National Commission on Urbanisation 1988 in Amjad 1990:131) women from urban slums definitely represent a large majority of Indian women who live at or below subsistence level. I believe it is important to learn about the birth control and sexual experiences of urban slum-dwelling women because of what it reveals about women's agency in this crucial, most intimate aspect of their lives. My preliminary questions initially led to a search for answers in available literature on the relationship, if any, between gender, class and income on the one hand, and sexual politics and birth control decision-making within the household, on the other.

FERTILITY OUTCOMES: DO GENDER, CLASS AND INTRAHOUSEHOLD DIFFERENTIALS MATTER?

Mainstream demographic research in India in the past three decades has dwelt on determinants of fertility outcomes: rationalizations for expanded family size (Mamdani 1973; Michaelson 1981); social structural aspects of limiting family size (Caldwell et al. 1988) and demographic correlates of reproductive behaviour (Pakrasi and Malakar 1967; Sandhu 1996). A common feature in these studies is the assumption that the household is a homogeneous unit, whose members are unanimously geared to take decisions on family size and/or maximization of utility regarding children. Differences in household members' desires and experiences, therefore, go unnoticed. The studies also largely ignore the issue of class.

At least part of the limitation of fertility research emanates from its overwhelming preoccupation with fertility outcomes: ideal family size, actual number of children, fertility rate and so on. While these factors are important they cannot really address certain issues related to women's agency in the reproductive process. For instance, the dynamics of sexual behaviour are closely related to childbearing. Population studies, however, have hardly explored how women in particular class and gender contexts negotiate in the sexual domain, what they think and feel about love, physical affection, sexual initiation and sexual satisfaction. We do not adequately know how subjective understandings of these issues help to create and/or perpetuate gender and class traits affecting women's and consequently their families' life chances in the long run.

Some socio-psychological behavioural studies, however, have underscored the significance of gender and class characteristics in fertility and birth control behaviour. For instance, Rainwater (1960) found that among a sample of couples in an urban area, family planning practices are hindered by male dominance, poor communication and modesty between husbands and wives. Other studies (Groat and Neal 1967; 1980; Chilman 1973) see poverty as generating a 'subculture' which breeds attitudes of alienation, passivity, ambivalence and fatalism and undermines motivation to control reproduction. Yet none of these studies adequately examine the reasons behind wives' acceptance of these asymmetrical exchanges. Specifically, the linkages between spousal differences in household income allocation and control and sexual and birth control behaviour are not explored.

Women's roles and their consequent effect on fertility outcomes gradually became a more significant area of study in the seventies. In a review article written during this time, Birdsall (1976) suggested that the conflation of economic or socioeconomic and social-psychological variables could provide a legitimate framework towards incorporating the gender variable in demographic studies.

In the nineties, emphasis on household dynamics, related to demand for children has brought issues of gender, class, sexual division of labour in the household and the macro-micro links in these relationships into sharper focus. Mazumdar and Sharma (1990:186), however, comment that the literature on women's status in India is still 'only minimally concerned with the power dimension of household structures that affect the allocation of labour, time and other resources within the family and so have yielded limited insights into the lives of . . . working class women.'

And yet, in Annapurna's case, this power dimension was crucial. It enabled her to stop having children but the type of control she could wield in order to achieve this end 'recomposed' her subordinate gender and class location. Annapurna did not passively accept her situation. In spite of all the hurdles that dominated her life, she was able to glean some kind of birth control information, network with other women with similar agendas and obtain a tubectomy. Thus, the same circumstances that were cause for her subjugation also contained certain elements which gave her the strength to make a reproductive choice.

The gender bias in contraceptive promotion has met with considerable censure since the seventies when the field of Women in Development came into being. One attempt at reparation resulted in the generation of studies set in developing countries that looked at gender differences affecting fertility outcomes (Birdsall 1976). Also, studies on the relationship between women's roles, their positions in the social structure, their labour force participation and their fertility outcomes gained currency (Anker, Buvinic and Youssef 1982; Cain 1981). Scholars began to discard the New Household economics' model of the monolithic household and looked at fertility decision-making as a gender disaggregated phenomena within the household (Bruce 1989). There is a growing acceptance that decision-making in the area of fertility and family planning is a complex psychological process involving cognitive and affective aspects of behaviour and an attempt has been made to examine its influence on contraceptive use (Singh 1984:281). Further studies have attempted to elicit the relationship between employment activities, autonomy and use of birth control (Dharmalingam and Morgan 1996) as also the linkage between contraceptive behaviour and women's economic power and individual control over choice of partner (arranged versus love marriage). These perspectives brought the need to study the process of reproductive decision-making in sharper focus showing how women may have high stakes but little freedom of choice in deciding the timing, number and sex of children (Bruce 1989: 981).

This process through which Annapurna articulated her choice of what birth control method to use, formed the core of my research interest. Remaining within the boundaries of the field of 'Women in Third World Development', I wanted to approach this study from the perspective of the woman's situation in the household. At the same time I wanted to be able to link the household processes to societal processes of class and gender formations.[1] My exploration of existing literature was found wanting on elucidating the ramifications of the intra-household power struggle. It is worthwhile to mention here that one of the major changes occurring in family planning propaganda is the use of concepts like 'choice', 'freedom' and 'autonomy' after the ICPD Cairo and Beijing meetings (Agnihotri Gupta 1996). But this approach still sees women as instrumental for their ultimate goal of population control. There has been an adoption of a holistic perspective on sexuality and reproductive health and rights in the official Draft Programme of Action prepared at Cairo and Beijing. However, the struggle for reproductive autonomy is closely related to other struggles against sexism, class and the market (ibid.). In this context, the Gender and Development (GAD) perspective offered some sort of theoretical framework within which I could initiate primary research.

GENDER AND DEVELOPMENT

The Gender and Development (GAD) perspective emanates from a socialist feminist approach: one which ascribes women's subordination and invisibility to an interplay of class and gender (Rathgeber 1990). This perspective gained attention as recently as the eighties as an alternative to liberal, radical and Marxist approaches to the study of Women in Development. The limitations inherent in the liberal, radical and Marxist approaches led Third World scholars and activists to develop a broader—more comparative—'socialist feminist' approach to women's development problems (Sen and Grown 1987). It grew from an effort to marry Marxist, liberal and radical feminist ideas in order to develop a model that considers both gender and class in explaining women's positions. Socialist feminists suggest that existing gender hierarchies place women 'in subordinate positions at each different level of interaction between class and gender' (Beneria and Sen 1981:290). This approach, as just mentioned, is referred to as GAD in current literature (Rathgeber 1990). On the one hand, the GAD approach draws from Marxist materialist methodology in its consideration of class inequalities. On the other hand, it incorporates issues of women's marginalization from production, patriarchy and social construction of gender from liberal and radical feminism.

To summarize, the Gender and Development (GAD) perspective takes a more holistic approach towards development (Young 1988). The proponents of this view argue that marginalization from the development process is not the only reason for women's subordination (Anand 1984). Rather, the phenomenon is ascribable to a variety of gender-related factors and patterns of economic growth systematically producing sharp class differences and social hierarchies (Beneria and Roldan 1987; Beneria and Sen 1982). Also, the approach tries to avoid 'androcentric and ethnocentric assumptions underlying development models' (Beneria and Roldan 1987:7). Thus, GAD proponents study Third World women within their specific historic and socioeconomic contexts. At the same time they avoid objectification of Third World women as a separate category and emphasize more comparative research underscoring the similarities and differences among the world's women (ibid.; Parpart 1989).

Despite the obvious advantages, there are some inherent limitations in the GAD approach. We need to keep them in mind while attempting any analysis based on the GAD premise. The limitations described here are drawn from Beneria and Roldan's book *The Crossroads of Class and Gender* on Women Homeworkers in Mexico City.[2] The authors assert that a simultaneous focus on gender and class potentially engenders dualistic analyses. 'The specificity of real life does not present itself in a dualistic manner but as an integrated whole, where multiple relations of domination/subordination (based on race, age, ethnicity, nationality, sexual preference) interact dialectically with class and gender relations' (p. 10). Thus, scientific and humanistic research is required to capture both the wholeness of social reality and the nuances of its different elements. Extant theories are still devoid of this holistic orientation. Consequently, the 'problem before us is to build a unifying theory and analysis in which material and ideological factors are an integral aspect of our understanding of economic and social reality' (ibid.).

Despite the inherent drawbacks of the GAD rubric, I found this approach best equipped to explore the women's sexual and birth control trajectories within the dynamics of their resource contribution and gender articulations in the household. Development research in India clearly indicates that the current pattern of economic development affects women asymmetrically. Specifically, those women located in the marginal castes, classes and regions are the worst affected in the process (Sen and Grown 1987). Both public and private spheres of working class women's lives are, therefore, under severe strain (Minault 1986).

With regard to the study, therefore, a GAD perspective is able to reveal how poor women go about their daily existence in a labour intensive, financially tight economy while simultaneously managing their sexual and birth control domains through processes which create and/or recreate societal class and gender contexts. With this broad theoretical outline in mind, I consider sexual relations and birth control careers as intrinsic to the dialectics of women's reproductive roles in the household. These experiences are, therefore, innately linked to women's productive and other socially reproductive roles as paid and unpaid workers, as wives, mothers, daughters and daughters-in-law within the household. The household, of course, is not considered a monolithic entity. Rather, the emphasis is on dissecting the *household unit* to reveal its internal hierarchies. At the same time the household's location within a particular socioeconomic context is recognized since that defines and constrains the attempts of individual men and women to carve out their own histories (ibid : 9). Having explored the circumstances within which women's sexual and birth control histories are created, the ramifications in terms of societal gender and class formation in general and women's position in particular is discussed. Implications in terms of Gender and Development policy formulations, specifically those geared to Family Planning are also considered.

Accordingly, I found myself in the slums of Calcutta searching for some answers. As a part of my primary research, my aim was to meet a cross-section of Indian women from the working class and to explore—through dialogues with them—the nature of their struggle to control their own bodies.

METHODOLOGY

Throughout the analysis, I have used fictionalized names of respondents in order to maintain their privacy. Usage of names personalizes the particular woman's situation and underscores the qualitative bent of the research.

DATA COLLECTION AND DATA MANAGEMENT

Questionnaire Construction

Due to the nature of the study, it was imperative to construct a questionnaire that would allow respondents to speak as candidly as possible about their concerns, specifically about their sexual and birth control experiences. The task was particularly difficult because there are currently very few studies in India that focus on the sexual lives of poor women. Social workers in the slums also warned that the women I was going to interview would be somewhat reticent about their birth control behaviour if I did not make them feel at ease. Moreover, the social workers gave no guarantees about information on sexual behaviour since this was something they rarely discussed with one another. During the survey, however, out of the 100 women I interviewed some refused to comment on some of the questions on sexual behaviour, though none abstained from answering all of them.

In constructing the questionnaire, the build-up and sequence of questions were crucial. The format included information on demographic, residential and general household characteristics in the first section and childhood work and educational characteristics in the second. Questions related to present income-earning status, household income and savings followed next. Information on housework and sexual division of labour in the household, recreation and leisure and kin networks comprise the fourth and fifth sections, respectively. From the sixth section onwards, questions relate to marriage, pregnancy, contraception, love and sex-related perceptions and experiences. Having tapped those issues, the questions merge into other facets of the relationship with the husband, namely, household decision-making, alcoholism, family violence; feelings about the slum environment and political parties; access to medical facilities; belief in God, in fate and in magical healing. Needless to say, all the issue areas tapped in the questionnaire are not included in this study. It was necessary to engage in a detailed dialogue where one issue followed 'naturally' from a previous one both in order to put respondents at ease and in order to get a holistic account of their lives.

The structured questionnaire contained both closed and open-ended questions and involved a considerable amount of probing on certain issues. English wordings of questions were adapted from standardized questionnaires of other studies and surveys (*General Social Surveys* 1991; *National Longitudinal Study of Youth* 1992; Cvetkovich and Lonner 1973). The first version was translated first into Bengali and then into Hindi with Urdu modifications (with professional help). This was done after consultation regarding the contents of the questionnaire and manner of questioning with a social worker who had extensive experience in talking to poor women in Calcutta. The translated draft was tested in a pilot study of ten Bengali and Urdu speaking slum-dwelling women. Some of the existing terms, specifically those describing sex and birth control, were changed according to the common parlance of the women. The final questionnaire consisted of 85 main questions with subsections (see Appendix).

Since the soundness of the data was entirely contingent upon the women's responses to the questions, I introduced some validity checks into the questionnaire. First, since one of the major criteria for the study was to explore birth control and sexual experiences of women of childbearing age, I made sure that the women concerned were still menstruating (barring those that were pregnant at the time of the survey), regardless of what their reported ages were. Moreover, respondents' reports of their age were corroborated with ration cards (where available), reported age at first marriage, and age at first pregnancy. Reports about engagement in paid work were also corroborated with questions on detailed descriptions of daily schedules and hours of paid and unpaid work.

Setting, Nature and Duration of Interviews

I conducted the interviews in all the three languages, namely Bengali, Hindi and Urdu, where applicable. Each interview lasted two to three hours. After initial introductions, the atmosphere eased and the interview took the form of an informal discussion. All the interviews were recorded on tape except in one case where the woman preferred that I did not record her voice.

Two factors influenced the actual process of interviewing: type of space/privacy and time available. The interviews were conducted mostly in the afternoons between 1 and 3 p.m. after women completed their morning shift work and fed their families. Sometimes women talked while rolling papars, cutting newspapers for paper bags or breast-feeding babies. A few interviews were also conducted in the evening between 7 and 9 p.m.

In cases where women had to keep working or tending children, interviews were conducted in the women's households. This was the most difficult interview setting. More often than not women would be simultaneously doing housework and/or home-based work, trying to concentrate on two or three different things while responding to questions. Some rooms were so crowded with children and other adult kin-women that we would almost whisper to each other while talking about matters related to sex and birth control. At other times men and women simply peered or went in and out of the room interrupting the interview in the process. Some interviews were also set up in 'clubs': tiny rooms where various community activities of the slums took place. Here, the Non-Governmental Organizations (henceforth, NGOs) ran their operations conducting lessons, feeding children, distributing medicines, and so on. Women came from their nearby households and the social workers emptied a corner of the club for us to talk, while classes continued. Sometimes, I could get the club rooms when they were empty. For many women, leaving their rooms to participate in an interview was extremely inconvenient because of all the things they constantly needed to take care of at home. In one instance, a woman left to serve lunch to her family and never came back. In another case, a woman was in constant fear that her husband would find out that she was not at home and would consequently beat her. Her fear was so pervasive that she kept looking in the direction of the road to see if her husband was coming and talked her daughters into keeping a vigil. Ultimately, she left without completing the interview. Both women were dropped from the survey. In some cases, I interviewed women in a room in my family's or friend's houses. This scenario afforded the utmost privacy.

I was aware that the variations in interview settings could possibly bias the conclusions. In order to prevent that from happening I made sure that no one listened to our conversations under any circumstances. Women also talked only when they were sure that no one except I was listening to them. In fact, the middle class houses were private in that they provided quieter surroundings. Women in these settings were not necessarily more at ease to talk about sex and birth control compared to those in different settings. Shy women in all settings were more reticent and women with lesser inhibitions talked under all circumstances, once they were sure that no one else was listening.

Besides the 15 cases where interviews were conducted in middle class households with closed doors and windows, the interviews took place amid din and noise. While we talked, children learned lessons and sang songs, loudspeakers blared popular songs and election speeches, buses and trains clamoured past and sewing machines whirred. The scenario, therefore, was far removed from text book 'norms' of one-to-one interview settings and required a lot of adaptation, cooperation and creative communication techniques to elicit responses.

Despite all the inconveniences, women came and spoke, sometimes even losing out on hours of work and, therefore, much-needed earnings. Many times, there were expectations among the women that the interviews were leading to something: jobs, advice about health, contraceptives and various other solutions to problems that plagued their daily lives. Of course, I had no panacea to offer. But that did not deter most of them from being interested or from trying to help clarify issues, because, as Rukeya simply put it, 'It's a relief, sometimes, to empty one's heart out!'

Translating, Transcribing, Coding and Computing Procedures

The one hundred interviews were completed in nine months. I translated the interviews into English again from Bengali, Hindi and Urdu and transcribed them on paper. A basic coding scheme based on factual information and types of responses was formulated. Variables generated thereafter were ascribed numerical, almost entirely nominal values. The numbers were copied on computer spreadsheets and uploaded on mainframe SAS software to generate aggregate results. This took another 12 months.

DATA ANALYSIS

The analysis may be looked upon as an exploratory case study. The uniqueness of case studies lies in the fact that they assist researchers' attempts at drawing valid inferences outside the laboratory setting, while simultaneously sharing the objectives of laboratory science. Moreover, instead of

> presenting . . . evidence in the context-independent manner of positivistic 'confirmation' (or even of post-positivistic 'corroboration'), it is presented . . . in extended networks of implications that (while never complete) are nonetheless crucial to its scientific evaluation (Campbell, in Yin 1984:7).

Thus, since case studies underscore the significance of context and linkages, their methodology is uniquely suited for a holistic comprehension of women's situations in the present study. Also, being embedded in the GAD perspective, the analysis tends to avoid direct objectification of women. Rather, I treat them as subjects in the study and attempt to understand the needs and realities as expressed by the women themselves. This too is facilitated by the subjective bent of exploratory and descriptive case study approach (Yin 1984:13). The basic framework of the analyses employed is adapted from Beneria and Roldan's (1987) research on women engaged in subcontracting in Mexico City. The same authors also worked with a small purposive non-random sample within the GAD perspective and their research, therefore, bears many structural similarities to the present one.

This book reveals many significant linkages through correlational and case historical analyses of data. The findings are strictly suggestive, in terms of their 'generalizability', but the issues raised and the methodology undertaken make a substantial contribution to the study of household dynamics in India. Overall, then, the methodology tries to address women's realities more holistically to see how women's sexual and birth control histories are created within the gender and class contexts in which they grow up and those they deal with in their daily lives. The present study is descriptive and exploratory, providing a foundation for further research. This, however, does not mitigate the significance of the study, because, representative or not, it tells a story of human lives that needs a hearing.

The statistics presented are in the form of percentages. Because of the nature of the sample, tests of significance are not relevant. Trends and linkages are described through frequency tables and cross-tabulations in terms of the magnitude of the percentages appearing in the cells. All the statistical descriptions in Chapters 4 and 5 are corroborated by some case histories to elucidate (*a*) aspects described in the quantified data and (*b*) non-quantifiable elements and complexities which cannot be represented in quantified aggregate data.

The following chapters, then, will elucidate various facets of the class and gender articulations inherent in women's resource contribution and control and gender division of labour within the household. These contexts are then linked to working class women's sexual and birth control trajectories. Chapter 1 will provide a description of the setting or context—physical, historical, political and ideological. Chapter 2 will elucidate various characteristics of the sample and compare these with the overall slum population of Calcutta. Chapter 3 will explore some of the dynamics of the women's position in the household vis-à-vis their husbands, in terms of the patterns and limits of control over household income and sexual division of labour. Chapter 4 focuses on the dynamics of conjugal sexual interactions and discusses the limits of women's renegotiation of gender relations drawing from the insights on household exchanges in the previous chapter. Chapter 5 examines women's experiences with birth control, again relating the patterns and limits of their negotiations to the household exchanges revealed in Chapter 3. Finally, the Conclusion summarizes the general patterns revealed and outlines their implications for further research, policy and action.

NOTES

1. The conceptualization of Gender and Class is similar to that of Beneria and Roldan (1987:11-13). Gender is regarded as a social and historical construct which places human beings in hierarchies on the basis of attributes and actions so that those connected with men are usually valued more. Gender hierarchies are articulated both at macro and micro levels of societal interactions and form the basis of societal award and resource allocations. The process and outcome of gender construction gives rise to normative expectations, different forms of subordination and struggles to do away with the subordination. Gender construction, however, occurs concomitant to formation of class, caste, race, ethnicity and other such relations. Accordingly, women's and men's perceptions and experiences of gender vary on the basis of their experiences in life.

   Like Beneria and Roldan's study (1987:13), this study opts for a Weberian 'cultural/historical' concept of class instead of a more reductionist structural Marxist precept. Thus, besides its historical relation to the economic underpinnings of society class is also seen as being related to 'coherent cultural existence, common social identity, and life styles, features expected to originate from shared historical experiences through generations.'
2. Much of the theoretical and analytical concepts of the present study are adapted from *The Crossroads of Class and Gender: Industrial Homework, Subcontracting, and Household Dynamics in Mexico City*, by Lourdes Beneria and Martha Roldan (1987). Hailed as a 'ground-breaking study of homeworkers in Mexico city' (Florence E. Babb, 1990:239 in *Latin American Research Review* 25(2): 236-47) this book is a 'mature by-product' of 'almost two decades of research, writing, and polemic on the question of women and development.' The book is also one of the first of its kind to empirically apply the Gender and Development frame work in a case study. In the process, it successfully links macro and micro levels of the economy and situates women as key actors in understanding these linkages (Deniz Kandiyoti 1989:939 in *Signs* 14:939-42).

   > The great virtue of the book is in identifying sympathetically and convincingly the strains to which low-income households and, in particular, the women within them are subject as a result of current patterns of economic growth in the developing world. Beneria and Roldan stress the need to include women's needs as expressed by women themselves in rethinking development policies. They have made a considerable contribution to this objective by publishing their study (Bryan Roberts, 1989:447 in *Economic Development and Cultural Change*, 37 : 447-449).

1

THE WORKING CLASS WOMAN IN CALCUTTA: HER CONTEXT

The primary research undertaken for this study consisted of interviews with a hundred women in fifteen slums across Calcutta. I will now discuss the general context of the female working class slum-dweller residing in Calcutta. An awareness of what makes up her backdrop will help us develop a more holistic understanding of her point of view.

We will begin with her physical surroundings followed by the historical origin of the urban slum in Calcutta. Among the many disaffected people who have contributed to the formation of the urban slum are working class women, who have been forced to eke out a living in the unorganized sector.

The slum-dwelling woman's experience of work in the unorganized sector is of relevance here. We can then touch on some of the gender socialization experiences to which these women are exposed at a formative young age and which tend to influence critically their life trajectories—limiting access to many opportunities available to their male counterparts, not least in the areas of education and employment. Finally, a description of India's National Family Planning Programme (which, being free, is the only means for these poor women to access birth control) brings us directly in touch with the avenue through which the working class slum-dweller negotiates sexual and birth control decisions.

LIFE IN AN URBAN SLUM: CALCUTTA

Calcutta, a few years ago, was, perhaps, the way it always will be. The ruling leftist state government had won yet another election and the city was fraught with opposition-led protests against price hikes and factory closures. Although the situation was not much different from the 'normal' pattern of the city's functioning, it was definitely exacerbated by the fact that the entire country was simmering with caste, communal and ethnic tensions. Spurred on by the Gulf War, mounting internal and external debt, a second election in eighteen months, India faced its worst fiscal crisis. Borrowings from the World Bank and the IMF increased India's debt burden to almost fourfold over the previous decade. Double digit inflation and tax hikes hit urban India much harder than rural (Guha Thakurta 1991; Bhimal and Jain 1992).

These growing economic crises naturally affected life in Calcutta, particularly in the city's slums. In fact, Calcutta is a city whose slums have often epitomized Third World poverty. Over the years, the Calcutta Metropolitan Development Authority and Calcutta Municipal Corporation have attempted to improve the slum situation by paving alleys, installing street lights, community hand pumps, taps, lavatory, sewerage, and health and education facilities (Calcutta Metropolitan Development Authority [CMDA] 1991). The quality of improvement and the targets achieved, however, continue to fall far short of desired standards (Nagchowdhury 1991). Calcutta, consequently, remains one of the poorest metropolitan cities in the world.

Unlike in New Delhi and Mumbai, where you do not find pockets of slums in the midst of affluent localities, Calcutta's slums are cheek by jowl with middle class areas. Living conditions in these slums leave much to be desired. Only four of the fifteen slums I visited had concrete roads and some street lighting. Two of the slums in the southern part of the city are located next to railway tracks. Children played, clothes dried, men smoked and women stitched while sitting on the tracks, only to be interrupted by an oncoming train. As a train thundered past they waited at a dangerously close distance to the roaring wheels, to resume their routines as soon as the train vacated their 'spaces' on the tracks. During the ten months that I visited these areas, two children died on the tracks since they could not get away in time. Other slums, in less perilous locations have no sewerage and garbage disposal facilities and become flooded during the monsoon rains.

With regard to civic facilities, an average of twenty to thirty families shared a tap or tubewell, a covered bathing space[1] and a lavatory. Most of the lavatories were dug-outs or sewer outlets with their lids removed and the space around covered with jute cloth for privacy; very few had septic tank sanitary facilities. There was no indoor plumbing and in most cases, no electricity. Water was scarce and it was common to see long lines of women and children waiting by a tap or tubewell with buckets and pots. Electricity too was scarce. Households with electricity could afford a maximum of only one table fan and one neon light and sometimes a black and white television. Radios were mostly battery operated.

Most of the indoor electricity installations were illegally connected to the main street circuits and these were most dangerous. Though not in the best of condition, all slums had some primary health care facility (mostly free or subsidized), including access to some birth control methods either in the area itself or in some nearby hospital or private clinic. Free primary schooling facilities through governmental and non-governmental organizations were available for the children. Lack of money to buy books and stationery was a disincentive to continue in school, however. Such problems were compounded by excessive unemployment and underemployment in almost every household.

But it wasn't just the women's surroundings that were squalid. One of the first things which struck me while talking to the women about their sexual lives was the appalling lack of privacy in which they had to live. In most cases, each family unit—ranging from twenty to one hundred square feet in floor area—was hardly separated from the next by a thin wall. Inside, the rooms had two- and/or three-tier arrangements. Typically, the floor constituted the cooking space. For domestic outworkers[2] it was also the working area. Cheap plywood beds (*chouki*) comprised the middle level. The bed was raised from the ground with three or four bricks. The area below the bed was used for sleeping, storing, changing clothes and other such activities. The top of the bed was obviously used as a sleeping area, rationed out to newborns and newlywed couples in extended households. In other instances, sons and daughters of women interviewed and some of the women themselves used the bed as a study area. In some rooms the roof was so low that it was impossible even for the children to sit straight in order to read or write. When roofs were high enough to accommodate a third tier, the area was used as a loft where the family valuables: secret savings in a mud pot, sequined saris worn once a year during festivals, wedding utensils and wall clocks were kept and cherished.

The daily events of the women's lives then, took place in cramped and dank rooms, alongside unpaved dusty roads, pools of dirty water, human waste and garbage which piled up for days on end with flies and mosquitoes hovering around them. Amidst these surroundings it was amazing that the women responded to me, a complete outsider, in the manner in which they did. Taking time off busy schedules, ignoring the glares of suspicious male 'guardians', pacifying wailing children, they talked about their respective childhood experiences, marital lives, frustrations and aspirations. Sometimes, the interviews had to be terminated midway because they could not give me the hours I needed. I had to visit them two or three times to complete my work, yet, all the time they were eagerly waiting and ready.

For ten months, I called on a hundred women amidst their squalid surroundings. With each passing day, I learnt to look at the city objectively for perhaps the first time in the first twenty-two odd years of my life here before I left Calcutta to study abroad. This 'objectivity' was not the patronizing kind that leads one to call Calcutta a 'City of Joy', nor was it the nagging guilt of feeling 'How could I have taken these appalling conditions so much for granted?' Rather this 'objectivity' bred a sense of curiosity to fathom how the sleepy villages that Job Charnock bought for a pittance in the seventeenth century became the Calcutta I was seeing today. How did Calcutta become a city where roughly one-third of its ten million people are housed in slums?

Conflict between the leftist party governing West Bengal over the past 22 years and the ruling party at the centre has contributed to a deadlock over trade, industry and labour policies and led to the flight of human and financial capital to other, more vibrant regions (S. Dasgupta 1992; GOI 1991; Chatterjee 1998). But the evolution of Calcutta as an epicentre of urban poverty far predates the Centre-state conflict era.

ORIGIN OF THE URBAN SLUM

Located on India's eastern coast, Calcutta thrived as a river port in the eighteenth and nineteenth centuries, serving British commercial and manufacturing interests (Standing 1985; CMDA 1991). As is typical with colonial policies, the British made no attempts to develop a strong agro-economic structure in Calcutta's hinterlands (Dasgupta et al. 1991). From the mid-eighteenth century British industrial capitalism initiated a process of disintegration of the Indian economy. The 'de-industrialization' of India which followed resulted in 'massive and irrevocable destruction' of Indian industries. Indian merchants were banned from buying from local producers. Instead, they had to purchase goods from the British East India Company and to function only as agents. In the process, a large majority of the urban and rural populations were reduced to poverty (Desai and Krishnaraj 1987:54-55).

For Calcutta and its hinterlands, a similar pattern of depletion emerged (Dasgupta et al. 1991; CMDA 1991). Farming of commercial crops like jute and indigo was enforced at the cost of food crop production and indigenous manufacturing in the surrounding rural areas lead to further impoverishment of the region (Datta 1984). Concomitantly, industries growing around these products were set up around Calcutta. As a result, working class villagers from the indigent hinterlands of eastern, central and northern India poured into the city in search of jobs in the eighteenth and nineteenth centuries (CMDA 1991). Moreover, land relations prevailing in most of northern, central and eastern India (including Bengal) were such that it benefited the administrative authorities and the non-cultivating revenue collectors (referred to as subedars, zamindars, and so on through different phases of Mughal and British rule) and undermined the well-being of small farmers who bore the major brunt of the land revenue taxes. The system of inequality was further entrenched with the introduction of the Permanent Settlement Act in 1793, according to which the zamindars/landlords were made to pay fixed revenue by the first of every month but were allowed to retain the right to increase their subjects' rent. Also, if and when a subject failed to pay the requisite rent, the zamindar executed his right to seize the property without any mediation of a court of law.

Consequently, between 1793 and 1880, tenants'/tillers' rents in all districts of Bengal increased from 120 percent to 180 percent. With increased scope of monetary earnings, the number of intermediaries increased and so did the burden of rent on peasants. Intermediaries like the zamindars were solely interested in collecting rent and neglected their responsibility of upgrading irrigation. This accelerated the decay of the agrarian system and pushed more peasants towards the industrially growing urban centres in and around Calcutta.

As these migrants settled down, 'native' mud, bamboo, ironsheet and tile huts sprouted in many sections of the city. They were in stark contrast to the urban grandeur of the 'European zone' whose architecture, planning and civic facilities were state-of-the-art replications of the buildings 'back home'. No efforts were made, however, to upgrade the weak civic infrastructure of the 'native' zones. The divide was so deep that to this day it has not been possible to integrate the locale lagging behind in terms of infrastructure with the 'European half' of the city (Dasgupta et al. 1991:iv; CMDA 1991). The huts in the 'native' zones were built and rented out by middlemen (*thikadars*) who leased land from the original landowners.[3] By the mid-eighteenth century, the huts grew in number and density (Desai and Krishnaraj 1987). These clusters, occupied by families sharing a lavatory without arrangements for water supply or drainage disposal, were the first slums (ibid.).

By the early twentieth century Calcutta had lost much of its strategic importance for the British with the growth of other, more convenient, sea ports in Bombay and Madras. In 1911, the British also moved their capital from Calcutta to Delhi in the north due to increasing nationalist activities which threatened the operation of the British government in the region (Myrdal 1986; Standing 1985). At the same time, however, textile, engineering and other industries emerged in the region. The growth of these industries led to the increased importance of the railway link from Calcutta to Calcutta Port.

These factors led to unbridled and somewhat haphazard urbanization of the city and migrants flowed in unabated, mainly from the states of Bihar, Uttar Pradesh, Rajasthan and Orissa. They joined the city's labour force as factory labourers, conservancy staff of Calcutta Corporation, Port labourers, rickshaw pullers, masons, plumbers and so on. The thirties saw a wave of people from eastern, central and northern India in search of manufacturing jobs created to support the war efforts of the British. The Partition of Bengal upon Independence in 1947, resulted in large scale migration from East Pakistan (now Bangladesh) and illegal immigration from Bangladesh has continued ever since (CMDA 1991; S. Dasgupta 1992). Thus, slums grew as more and more poor migrants settled in the low lying vacant lands in the city. Living conditions deteriorated (CMDA 1991; Datta 1984) as the government found it impossible to set up an urban policy and upgrade the already weak civic infrastructure (Dasgupta et al. 1991).

The post-war depression in Calcutta since the fifties resulted in industrial stagnation leading to the gradual decline of Calcutta Port, as well as the jute, textile, chemical and engineering industries (Standing 1985; Diptesh Banerjee 1984). Meanwhile, population continued to expand. The predominant tertiary and unorganized sector which emerged, generated trade, commerce, transport, storage and other services, but offered mostly unproductive, non-remunerative and low-paid jobs to the migrants who still poured into the city due to persistent poverty in the hinterlands (Datta 1984; Desai and Krishnaraj 1987; *Ananda Bazaar Patrika* 1991). As a result, proliferation of slums continued unabated. The structures varied from bamboo and tile houses, to concrete wall and tin roof tenements, to two-/three-storey tenements (CMDA 1991).

All in all, restricted economic opportunities coupled with unbridled urban crowding have resulted in the current situation: one out of every three persons in Calcutta lives in slums where basic civic amenities are under serious strain (*Ananda Bazaar Patrika* 1991; B. Dasgupta et al. 1991). Slums have become a permanent feature of the city, to the extent that all development programmes aim for 'slum development' rather than 'slum clearance' which, admittedly, is not possible anymore (CMDA 1991; *Ananda Bazaar Patrika* 1991).

WOMEN'S EXPERIENCE OF WORK IN THE UNORGANIZED SECTOR

Although British manufacturing and trading practices beginning in India in the mid-eighteenth century destroyed and displaced indigenous artisan classes, the latter were not absorbed into new industries. Actually, most workers who were displaced and consequently unable to find a place in the new production units were women. This happened because women artisans were mostly involved in household-based production. The new production units, however, had moved to factories. Since women were responsible for housework and childcare, society expected them to fulfil this responsibility. This fact, combined with the existence of protective industrial policies, made it difficult for women to go out of their homes and work in factories. Thus, development through training and acquiring of skills in factory-based production systematically excluded women. Indeed, due to labour-related policies and women's domestic responsibilities, the structure of female employment in India remained almost unchanged in the five decades of growth oriented economic planning following Independence. Overall, factory-based industrialization has altered the employment structure to the extent that male labour has replaced female labour in most organized sectors of industries.

Also, concomitant to the stagnant condition of women's employment, India's organized sector also started acquiring a stagnant character in the post-Independence years. The import-substitution industrialization model which India adopted, proved to be inadequate in terms of generating growth and national income (Baud 1992). The overabundance of labour left at bay by an inadequate development model naturally generated an informal economy where highly competitive and exploitative conditions facilitated the growth of capital (Mathew 1992; Omvedt 1992). Consequently, restructuring towards an export-oriented industrial model led to changes in labour market segmentation, resulting in subcontracting of production among larger groups of people (Baud 1992).

Discrepancy between supply and demand for labour similarly affected the Calcutta labour market. The influx of refugees and already deteriorating economic conditions created a severe employment crisis in the city (N. Banerjee 1985). The evolving economy presented a paradoxical situation for women. On the one hand, inflation, growing male unemployment and underemployment necessitated earning a family wage. On the other hand, displacement from the organized sector and systematic de-skilling placed them below men seeking employment. The obvious choice for a large number of unskilled and restricted women, therefore has been 'the dregs of the job market' in the unorganized sector over the past twenty years (ibid.: 147). These women, thus, joined the economy as impoverished members of the subproletariat.

Like the proletariat, the subproletariat lacks ownership and control over the means of production. The major difference between the two is that the subproletariat is located in the unorganized sector and therefore lacks protected wages and benefits coverage. Forms of remuneration range from casually agreed upon cash compensation to non-cash items like food and shelter. There are no formal long-term contracts and the unstable wages may lead members of this class to participate in more than one income-generating activity at the same time. The relative stability of jobs and benefits received therein give proletarian workers and presumably, their households more long- and short-term financial security than subproletarian workers and their households.

It is worthwhile to mention here that in order to better elucidate the gender dimensions of subproletarian class placement, I categorize class on the basis of sectors:

(*a*) General waged subproletariat. This includes individuals employed in public or private undertakings that 'stand a better chance of graduating into the ranks of the proletariat' (Beneria and Roldan 1987:77). In the context of Calcutta, it includes individuals in small scale units or sweatshops making cycle tubes, bottles, bottle caps, plastic bags, biris and sewerage pipes and service units engaged in binding books, repairing cars, running elementary schools, catering and decorating and selling meat and confectioneries.

(*b*) Subproletariat in skilled task-based services. In contrast to the former's monthly wages, they are paid more often in terms of hourly rates and commissions. It includes those hired on assignment basis to work as masons, private bus drivers and ticket collectors, house painters, rickshaw pullers, machine operators and tailors and remunerated through commissions and hourly/daily/piece rates. Also, there is a greater degree of variation in incomes in this group depending upon the type of specialization and the demand and supply of the service (e.g., operating a three wheel rickshaw is a skill-oriented task, but is regarded as something that all 'men' can learn with practice. Consequently, commission rates can be very low).

In contrast to the two groups just described, the following four groups have little economic stability and therefore less opportunities to move into the ranks of the proletariat:

(*c*) Autonomous subproletariat offering services or selling commodities in the market independently (ibid.:78). This pertains to those selling grain, vegetables, fruits, betel leaf, cigarettes, biri and cooked food, fuel wood, those making clay and iron items and paper bags and ironing stand operators in this sample.

(*d*) Subproletariat offering personal services. Individuals working for private consumers as part-time domestic help.

(*e*) Subproletariat in home-based subcontracting. These are individuals engaged in work subcontracted out from manufacturing units. In this study, this consists of individuals rolling biris and papads, sewing gloves, assembling boxes and accessories and pasting envelopes and files.

(*f*) Subproletariat in seasonal/temporary agricultural and non-agricultural services. In the agricultural sector, the group includes casual agricultural laborers engaged in weeding, ploughing, winnowing, threshing, poultry and cattle-supervising work (some of the parents and adult relatives of women in the sample). In the non-agricultural sector, the categorization pertains to individuals involved in remunerative activities ranging from digging, delivering goods to running errands, whenever available (similar to Omvedt 1992; Baud 1992: 22-23 describing processes of working class formation in India; Mukhopadhyay and Savithri 1998).

Differences in employment guidelines and security between the formal proletariat and unorganized subproletariat sectors generate class-based differences in societal resource accumulation, occupational stability and household resource contribution between individuals placed in them. Gender-related factors may further compound these differences. This is of relevance when one considers that in general wage labour and higher wages seem to increase working class women's bargaining power (Baud 1992)—a trend also observed in industrialized western societies (England and Farkas 1986). In particular, there is some evidence in India and other Third World countries that relatively lower pooled income in the household engenders a greater role of the sex/gender systems in the division of food, health care, and education (Baud 1992: 295; Safilios-Rothchild 1980: 30; Qadeer 1998).

GENDER-BASED SOCIALIZATION

We spoke earlier about women being socialized to take care of household matters. Extant research suggests that much of an individual's socialization and accumulation of societal resources are shaped by the material and ideological domains of his or her household of origin (Papanek 1990). Material and ideological domains of households, in turn, are related to societal processes of class and gender formation. What then, were the material and ideological domains of the women's households of origin? How did this affect the women's educational, paid work, housework and marital trajectories? What role did gender play in influencing the class-related experiences of the women in their households of origin?

A woman's life stage of origin is an important determinant of her future. Essentially, 'origin' refers to the social class context in which she was brought up. The shaping of the social class of all the women I interviewed began in their pre-marital households, that is, their households of origin. Their social class can be partially ascribed to the kind of physical and social environment in which they were brought up, and partially, to the social class of their family members, particularly, the heads of their households. Related to this are elements of social class that are acquired, such as, most obviously: education.

I have chosen the time when the women were ten to eleven years old to evaluate a woman's life stage of origin—the rationale being that:

> at this time the educational future has been decided for most of the women interviewed. If the woman has already begun formal education during this period, it is decided whether she will complete elementary school, begin her paid occupational trajectory (if she has not begun already) or devote her time to household chores, making it easier for other family members to work outside the home. (Beneria and Roldan 1987: 79)

One of the critical areas on which gender-based socialization has an impact, is in the sphere of education. The underlying ideology which influences the level of education of the girl child is overwhelmingly affected by gender norms operating under circumstances of poverty. According to these norms, a daughter's future is directed towards becoming a wife and mother. Educating her before she moves into her in-laws' household is seen as useless, if not detrimental to her future prospects since (*a*) it would require her to find a husband who is more educated than she; and (*b*) as a housewife, she is perceived as not having much opportunity to use her education, anyway. Whereas education for the male is viewed as an investment, education of the female is seen as a luxury few in the subproletariat can afford. Daughters are, instead, expected to help their mothers with household chores, care of younger siblings and, wherever possible, work in the unorganized sector to add to a meagre family income.

In this context, Basu (1992) notes that the prevailing kinship system, low economic productivity and high non-economic physical seclusion, which emanates out of a predominantly male domestic and public power structure in India, leads to devaluation of females both as children and as adults. Ironically, this leads to internalization of devalued social worth in the household among women themselves. Consequently, even the control over resources leads women selectively to favour boys over girls. Differences in entitlements to resource shares experienced from childhood and reinforced as adults, help shape self-perceptions on the basis of gender and class (Papanek 1990; Mukhopadhyay and Savithri 1998; UNDP 1998).

Thus, educational level in the 'older childhood phase' invariably predetermines the future of the girls concerned. A combination of lower levels of education and lower sense of self-worth vis-à-vis their male counterparts, perpetuates women's position of disadvantage over men into future generations. This is borne out by the fact that even if a woman in the working class is employed, she is likely to be so only in the unprotected unorganized sector, as just discussed earlier. In other words, low levels of education (predetermined by gender socialization) and unstable employment (also partially predetermined by gender socialization and further compounded by low levels of education) work side by side in a vicious circle to subjugate generation after generation of working class slum-dwelling women. In spite of these oppressive circumstances, these women (and Annapurna is a primary case in point) manage to carve out limited areas of influence and control, through overt and covert negotiation, within their respective households. I focus on the quality of this negotiation in the sexual and birth control arena, and turn now to an overview of India's National Family Planning Programme, which, being free, is the only means through which members of the subproletariat can afford to make birth control choices.

INDIA'S NATIONAL FAMILY PLANNING PROGRAMME

The Family Welfare Programme in West Bengal (and in India) promotes two types of female sterilization methods: (*a*) tubectomy (or tubal ligation), a permanent method of birth control for women, requiring hospitalization; and (*b*) laparoscopic female sterilization, a permanent method of birth control requiring a surgical operation and no hospitalization (Department of Health and Family Welfare, Government of West Bengal 1986 : 30). Other birth control methods include male sterilization (vasectomy), medical termination of pregnancy (MTP, implying abortion), the pill (Mala or Mala-D, the brands promoted and distributed by the programme), intra-uterine devices (IUD, includes Loop and Copper T), condom (Nirodh, government's brand), rhythm, withdrawal and abstinence.

India's National Family Planning programme launched in 1951 has been largely female-centric in that women have to take the major responsibility for effective birth control use. Women, therefore are considered reproductive agents who, if made to accept birth control, can assuage the threat of India's growing numbers (Chanana 1989; Joseph 1992; Agnihotri Gupta 1996; Manna 1998). This pattern is in line with the global trend in development policies which offered an interesting anomaly to poor women in the Third World since the fifties. While for the most part, programmes related to food production, income generation and education lost sight of them (Boserup 1970); policies for 'population control' easily identified poor women as the target group. These women could help reduce birth rates and expedite the process of economic growth if they were made to accept contraception (Desai and Patel 1989; Borooah et al. 1985; Gupta Agnihotri 1996; Manna 1998). Annapurna's tubectomy was part of this trend. Her case now is one in the statistics pertaining to 'Sterilization Targets Achieved'.

Female sterilization has been the pervasive and growing form of birth control in India (Aslam 1992; Desai and Krishnaraj 1987; Mukhopadhyay and Savithri 1998). This is so despite criticisms from scholars and practitioners regarding its relative inefficacy in relation to other birth control methods. First, in comparison to vasectomy, the male sterilization method, female sterilization, whether it is tubectomy or laparoscopic sterilization is more expensive and hazardous to health (Basu 1985; Chatterjee 1989; Mukhopadhyay and Savithri 1998). Second, since it is terminal and irreversible it is not the most effective method choice in a society where the survival rate of children is still low (Desai and Krishnaraj 1987). For instance, a woman in the sample lost her second child after having undergone sterilization. She regretted her decision and constantly blamed herself. Third, sterilization becomes an option for women, only after they have had a specified number of children (ibid. 1987). Consequently, it prevents birth-spacing and leads to deterioration of the mother's health and population growth (Basu 1985; M. Chatterjee 1989). A female-centric contraceptive culture, thus, places the onus of contraception on women without being sensitized to their life situations (Prakash 1991; Nair 1992).

Besides underscoring the 'insensitivity' of Family Planning programmes, studies have questioned the effectiveness of women-centred family planning practices in highly patriarchal milieus where women's low family status may be a deterrent to fertility control (Dyson and Moore 1983). In a study on household health status of poor rural women, Meera Chatterjee (1989:183) points out that: 'it is nowhere more evident that women are caught between traditional norms and practices and inadequate state policies than in the area of family planning.' Why is the Indian government continuing to promote female sterilization in spite of its disadvantages? According to critics, the family planning programme in India promotes tubectomy or laparoscopic sterilization over other methods (despite its declared 'cafeteria approach' where clients can choose whichever form of contraception they want) since the latter require education and monitoring and are therefore much more cumbersome than inducing women to terminate child-bearing once and for all (see Basu 1985; Desai and Krishnaraj 1987). Thus, although the onus of contraception is vested on women, they are not adequately informed about the available methods (Basu 1984; Agnihotri Gupta 1996).

Additionally, forced male sterilization undertaken during the Emergency or suspension of democracy (1975–76) led to a backlash against vasectomies. Instead, the family planning programme has greatly relied upon female sterilization (and other female-centred contraception) and neglected male sterilization (and other male-centred methods) in order to attain reasonable overall acceptance rates (Basu 1985: 422). In the process, the limitations of female sterilization have been ignored. Moreover, critics have started questioning whether the individual hazards of female sterilization may be overlooked by family planning authorities because the bulk of the clientele for this method are poor women (ibid.: 425).

Thus, Basu (1992) asserts that acceptance of sterilization among women in India may be more a function of the government's role in promoting tubal ligation as the main method of fertility control than the role of women themselves. Consequently, usage of non-terminal contraception and sterilization of spouses of women in the peak sterilization age group of 30–49 are more indicative of women's agency and control over contraception than female sterilization itself.

Regarding male attitudes towards vasectomy, studies demonstrate that men's unwillingness to obtain sterilization is a response generated as a result of the backlash to forced male sterilizations which took place during the Emergency, as mentioned earlier (Aslam 1992; Narayana and Kantner 1992). Other studies focus on more culturally ingrained factors that operate within a patriarchal system. By refusing to obtain sterilization men can feel safe and superior with their virility, the loss of which they dread (D. Banerjee 1971; Dubey and Bardhan 1975).

Journalistic reports examining male attitudes to contraception in India show that men tend to be more concerned with sexual gratification per se and less interested in contraception. In fact, urban Indian males offering to take the onus of contraception on themselves are rare (Dutt et al. 1992; Barnett and Stein 1998). This trend is further exacerbated by the fact that policy-makers and the medical community show little interest in developing male-centred contraceptives (Dutt et al 1992; Joseph 1992). Moreover, female-centred contraceptives befit male desires, wants and needs instead of those of women (Roberts 1981; Patel 1990).

Policy planners often fail to consider these complexities while implementing their strategies. For instance, the KAP (Knowledge, Attitude and Practices of Family Planning) surveys showed, that on the average, the number of children borne by Indian women was much greater than the women's desired family size (Gittlesohn et al. 1994; Dixon-Mueller 1996).

Policy-makers ascribed this difference between the desired and actual family size to women's lack of access to effective contraceptives (ibid.). On the basis of this understanding, the markets in less developed countries were swamped with contraceptives for women's use. In the long run, however, fertility rates remained high (*Health on the March* 1996-97) because, in fact, there was and is more to the issue than mere access.

Overall, then, the performance of the Indian Family Planning

Programme draws two main types of criticism. One, adhering to the modernization school, critiques the centrist bureaucratic model of the programme as an expression of a tradition-bound soft state unable to adapt to the efficiency ethic of contemporary times (Narayana and Kantner 1992). The other source of criticism, Marxist in its proclivities, asserts that much more than the operation of the programme itself, it is its quality that needs restructuring. These critics contend that the failure of the family planning programme is due in large part to its anti-natal ideology which professes to 'control' birth and consequently imposes governmental policies on people instead of giving them viable choices to determine their reproductive behaviour (A.R. Desai 1980; Demerath 1976; D. Banerjee 1971; Ramanathan 1998). Indeed, the Marxist critics suggest that the programme only pays lip service to providing a variety of methods (A.R. Desai 1980). In reality choices are restricted by inadequate facilities and information, preventing usage of reversible methods and concomitant promotion of few selected methods, specifically terminal, irreversible methods by the government (ibid.; D. Banerjee 1971; Prakash 1991; Basu 1984; Nair 1992; Joseph 1992; Agnihotri Gupta 1996).

The evaluation of the family planning programme performance, however, is not within our purview. Rather, the aim has been to furnish a general impression about constraints faced by the women in getting information about and services for birth control methods offered by the programme. Within that framework it will suffice to say that these women are also affected and constrained by the dynamics of extant family planning services. Additionally, the programme's orientations serve to further exacerbate the gender politics in contraceptive usage.

This was the backdrop against which I began to fathom the unfolding life situations of the women I met.

NOTES

1. Men and children usually bathe at the public water outlets on the streets. Women tend to use the covered spaces. However, since the covered spaces are inadequate, women often bathe on the streets as well.
2. These are the women doing home-based remunerative work. The goods they assembled were subcontracted out from larger manufacturing units either directly to the women or through agents.
3. Land prices in the Calcutta Metropolitan area went up significantly in the post-World War II period. Landlords at this time tried to evict the thikadars or middlemen and renters and sell land at higher prices. The government intervened to protect the renters and thikadars. Gradually, the landlords lost interest in the upkeep of the sanitary facilities in the slums. The landowner-thikadar-renter arrangement prevails to this day. In some cases, renters have bought the huts permanently. The West Bengal Thika Tenancy Act providing legal protection to slum dwellers against eviction was passed in 1981 (CMDA 1991: 3).

2

A History of Faces

"From the time I opened my eyes and learnt to see, I saw this slum, this railway track, these tiled roofs, the rich peoples' houses all around. I have not seen any other place. My friends live in bustees [slums] like these—bustees are our homes— I don't think I can live anywhere else."

I was hoping to interview at least one hundred women from slums in different parts of Calcutta. Within a few hours of knowing them, I was planning to ask them questions about very private events in their lives. It was an ambitious plan and, once begun, I quickly realized that the amount of time and monetary resources available to me would not facilitate a representative random selection of respondents, which is why the sample in this study is purposive, non-random. Despite its non-random nature, three factors help to validate the comparability of this sample with slum dwelling women in Calcutta:

(*a*) Non-Governmental Organizations (NGOs), recognized as being involved in slum development work helped in the selection of respondents;
(*b*) CMDA officials corroborated the slum area selection;
(*c*) the general demographic characteristics of Calcutta's slum dwellers (as depicted by Som 1987 which remains the most comprehensive data available on socioeconomic characteristics of Calcutta's slum dwellers) correspond to that of women in the sample.

I built up contacts with many NGOs actively involved in slum development schemes in different parts of the city. They were able to put me in touch with women from fifteen slums spread across the northern, central, southern and eastern parts of the city. At that time, political tensions had made mostly Muslim-dominated slum areas in the west inaccessible. Accessirig women through appropriate NGOs not only helped ease the women's wariness to

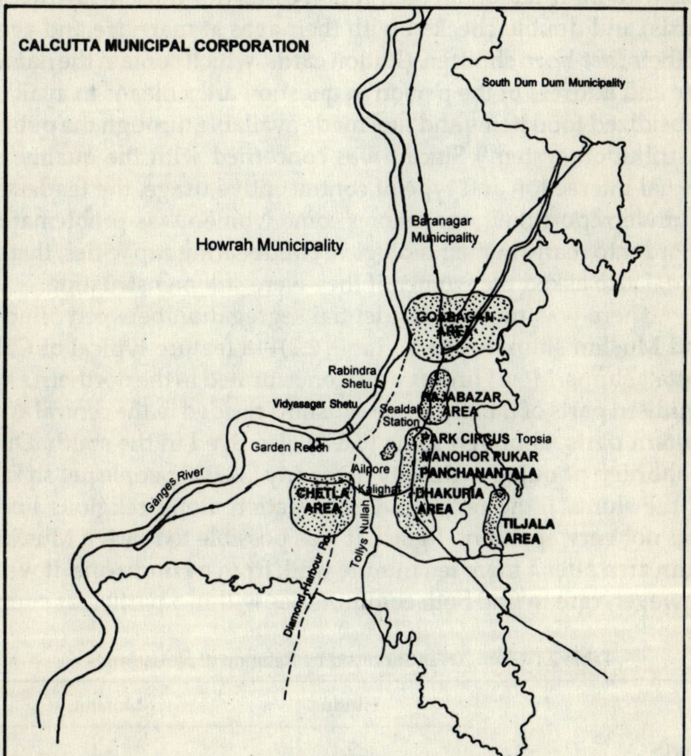

Figure 2.1: Map of Calcutta showing slum areas

talk to me but also assured me that the respondents came from areas which were 'recognized' and 'established' as typical slums (a fact later corroborated by officials at the CMDA). The market areas on the map of Calcutta Metropolitan Area indicate the general location of the slum areas.

I worked with one hundred women of childbearing age. I considered the reported ages of the respondents, corroborated this with information on their ration cards (for those who owned cards) and double-checked with their ages at marriage and ages of their first-born children. (Ration cards, which contain the name, age and address of the person in question are a means to avail of subsidized food items and fuel made available through the public distribution system.) Since I was concerned with the quality of sexual interaction and type of contraceptive usage, the tendency to underreport their age among some women was problematic. In order to reaffirm their biological childbearing capacities, therefore, I also asked the women if they were still menstruating.

There was marked residential segregation between Hindu and Muslim slum dwellers (Table 2.1)—a feature typical of Calcutta's slums. Most Hindus were concentrated in the northern and southern parts of the city while Muslims resided in the central and eastern parts, although some (8.8%) also lived in the south. Due to the high population density in the city (32,000 people per sq km in the slums[1]), the residential segregation along religious lines was not very apparent. In fact, it was possible to reach a Muslim slum area after a mere ten minute walk from a Hindu one. It was, however, rare to find both communities within a particular slum.

Table 2.1 Slum Areas Surveyed by Religion of Households

	Hindu	Muslim
North	39.4 (26)	- -
Central	1.5 (1)	55.9 (19)
East	1.5 (1)	35.3 (12)
South	57.6 (38)	8.8 (3)
Total (n)	100.0 (66)	100.0 (34)

As Table 2.1 reveals, 66 percent of the respondents came from Hindu households and the remaining 34 percent were Muslim. The total population of Calcutta is composed of 84.1 percent Hindus and 14.8 percent Muslims (Census of India, 1991). Focusing on the slum population, 72.9 percent is Hindu, while 28.9 percent is Muslim (Som 1987:155). Overall, then, the study sample largely corroborates the predominant religious groupings in Calcutta's slums, while slightly oversampling the minority group. The majority of respondents in Hindu households spoke Bengali (86.4%) followed by a Hindi-speaking group (13.6%). Among Muslims, the majority again spoke Urdu (88.2%) followed by a Bengali-speaking group (11.8%).

As far as duration of stay is concerned, there is a difference between the realities of men and women. For instance, women in my sample typically had one of two experiences. She may have entered an already existing slum household[2] as a bride (*bou*) or, arriving in Calcutta from her village or from another slum, she may have set up a slum household with her husband and/or marital/natal kin and children. In the first case, the slum household of the women's marital kin may have existed years before she entered the household as a bride. For that particular woman, however, the length of stay in the slum only spans the number of years she has lived in the household. Consequently, it should be kept in mind that the timing of a women's entry into a slum (which has been documented for the purpose of this study) may or may not coincide with that of her 'family'. The majority (80%) of the households had existed for more than five years. A small minority (16%) reported having lived in their households for three to five years. Only 4 percent reported their length of stay as less than a year. In order to ascertain their place of origin, I asked women (and their husbands) about their place of birth along with that of their parents. Fifty-three (out of 100) women reported being born in Calcutta. These women were second and third generation slum dwellers whose parents came from Bihar, UP, Orissa, East Pakistan (now Bangladesh) and from other districts of West Bengal. The rest (47%) were first generation occupants. A higher percentage of Muslims (88.2%) reported having been born in Calcutta compared to Hindus (34.8%). Thus, in this sample there are more second and third generation respondents among Muslims than among Hindus. The same was true for the husbands in the sample. Som (1987:156) notes that the largest percentage of Calcutta's slum dwellers come from other districts of West Bengal followed by Bangladesh, Bihar, UP, Orissa and some other states. The sample revealed similar characteristics. Based on these factors, it is fair to suggest that the sample is reasonably representative of Calcutta's slum-dwelling women.

Table 2.2 Distribution of Wives by Class and Head of Household of Origin

	Head of Household			Total
	Father	Mother	Other	
Informal Petty Bourgeoisie	13.2 (10)	- -	25 (1)	11 (11)
Proletariat	19.7 (15)	- -	- -	15 (15)
Subproletariat				
General Waged	14.5 (11)	5 (1)	- -	12 (12)
Skilled-task based	11.8 (9)	- -	- -	9 (9)
Personal Service	- -	50 (10)	- -	10 (10)
Autonomous	26.3 (20)	20 (4)	25 (1)	25 (25)
Home-based subcontracting	2.6 (2)	5 (1)	- -	3 (3)
Casual / Seasonal	11.8 (9)	20 (4)	50 (2)	15 (15)
Total (n)	100.0 (76)	100.0 (20)	100.0 (4)	100.0 (100.0)

*Adapted from Beneria and Roldan (1987: 81)

GENDER SOCIALIZATION AMONG RESPONDENTS

As discussed in Chapter 1, we have looked at each woman's socioeconomic status at the age of 10 to 11 in order to place her in a particular class: her life stage of origin. This criterion is relevant for most of the women in this study except for the fact that five of them were married before age eleven. None of these five girls, however, went to her marital household until gauna[3] which was not until five to seven years after marriage, so we can reasonably assume that marriage did not change her situation in the household of origin. It could have influenced her schooling, since marriage did restrict mobility. As one woman exclaimed, 'going to school after marriage was unheard of!' Four out of five of these girls never went to school. The fifth, Saima, received less than two years of education at home while she was being taught to read the Koran. The teaching stopped once she got married.

As revealed in Table 2.2, a majority of the heads of households are fathers (76%) with a diverse set of occupations, including those that put them in relatively better off sectors of the proletariat and petty bourgeoisie. Mothers and other female relatives, on the other hand, are solely grouped in the subproletariat with the largest concentration being in the relatively unstable personal service sector.

Table 2.3 Comparison between Occupation of Mother and Respondent

Mother	Daughter							
Subproletariat	1	2	3	4	5	6	7	Total
1. General - Waged	-	-	-	-	-	-	100.0 (1)	100.0 (1)
2. Autonomous	-	57.1 (4)	-	14.3 (1)	-	-	28.6 (2)	100.0 (7)
3. Personal Service	-	5.0 (1)	35.0 (7)	10.0 (2)	20.0 (4)	-	30.0 (6)	100.0 (20)
4. Home-based Sub-contracting	-	16.7 (1)	-	50.0 (3)	16.7 (1)	-	16.7 (1)	100.0 (6)
5. Casual / Seasonal (Agricultural Labourer)	-	11.1 (2)	55.6 (10)	-	5.6 (1)	-	27.8 (5)	100.0 (18)
Other								
6. Unpaid housework only	-	14.0 (6)	18.6 (8)	11.6 (5)	-	-	55.8 (24)	100.0 (43)
7. Not Applicable (Dead)	-	20.0 (1)	-	-	20.0 (1)	-	40.0 (2)	100.0 (4)

From Table 2.3, it is clear that, a generation later, daughters' employment patterns overwhelmingly reflect that of their mothers. The only major exception is that daughters of mothers who were agricultural labourers, mostly became domestic servants in the urban sector. In this case, although the sector of occupation had changed, the subordinate nature of the occupation had not. Thus, women growing up in male-headed households did not seem to have any advantage over their counterparts in female-headed households, in terms of access to better occupations. Irrespective of the nature of their households of origin, all the women ended up in unstable occupations with limited options or with no occupations at all, just as their mothers had.

Table 2.4 Wife and Husband : Literacy and Years of Education

	Wife			Husband		
	Hindu	Muslim	Total (n)	Hindu	Muslim	Total (n)
Literacy						
Literate	-	-	53 (53)	-	-	73 (73)
Illiterate	-	-	47 (47)	-	-	27 (27)
Total (n)	-	-	100.0 (100)	-	-	100.0 (100)
Years of Education						
0	43.9 (20)	52.9 (27)	47 (67)	22.7 (15)	35.3 (12)	27 (27)
1-4	28.8 (19)	38.2 (13)	32 (32)	15.1 (10)	17.6 (6)	16 (37)
5-10	27.4 (18)	8.8 (3)	21 (21)	37.9 (25)	35.2 (12)	37 (37)
11+	-	-	-	1.5 (1)	11.6 (4)	5 (5)
Don't Know	-	-	-	22.7 (15)	-	15 (15)
Total (n)	100.0 (66)	100.0 (34)	100.0 (100)	100.0 (66)	100.0 (34)	100.0 (100)

As observable in Table 2.4, almost half the wives are illiterate. Among the 53 literate wives, only one woman went as far as Class 10, but could not take the school-leaving examination. Thus, women in the sample have very low levels of education, if at all, and the trend does not change when they are compared across religion. As Naima reflected:

> I used to go out to wash utensils at the street tap and to watch the girls come out from the high school dressed in pretty red and white uniforms. I used to look at them and wonder what they did in their huge classrooms, what pictures they saw in their books, what they were learning that I would never have the opportunity to learn because I was poor and a girl.

In contrast to the wives, a majority of the husbands had completed at least five to ten years of education. Interestingly, a substantial number of women (15%) did not know the actual years of education of their husbands even though they knew their literacy status. During the interviews, these women typically replied to the questions regarding their husbands' education level by saying, 'Oh, I do not know, he can read some, sign his name and do some maths. That's all that matters. I never really felt the need to ask!'

The gender dimension of educational achievement becomes more evident when average years of education received by the respondents is compared to that of their brothers. While brothers on an average had six years of education (crossing primary level; a conservative estimate since many were still in school), the mean years of education received by respondents was 3.9 years. The situation was reversed when it came to doing housework: only 3.1 percent of respondents' brothers did housework while 98 percent of all girls did the same. Most women felt this was natural as Mitul's comment conveys,

> Of course my brothers went to school—they will grow up and earn—you can't expect them to do housework. Even when they wanted a glass of water, I had to get it for them.

I must point out here that all literate women did not necessarily go to school. Literate Muslim women who did not go to school acquired their reading and writing skills in Urdu, while being taught to read the Koran by female tutors at home. This is a common practice in Muslim households where religious decree inadvertently serves to infuse some cursory reading and writing skills. The female tutors themselves, however, are not very well educated and may have only studied up to Class 5. For instance, two Muslim women, who had studied through Class 7, earned money by teaching the Koran to female children in the neighbouring slum areas.

Among literate Hindu women, those who did not go to school picked up some reading and writing skills as children while working as part-time domestic helpers in middle class houses. In both the foregoing instances, the training was intermittent and short, not lasting more than two/three years. These respondents are regarded as having less than five years of education, though the content may not have been identical to that of a formal schooling system.

Such a state of minimal educational achievement was a constant source of pain and humiliation for the women. Maloti echoed their feelings when she lamented: 'Although we have eyes, we are blind!' Schooling expectations among the women were not very high. They only wanted to acquire functional reading, writing and arithmetic skills to help them get by. At the time of the survey, Maloti and other women like her were making serious efforts to fit in at least one hour of learning time in their daily schedules. Six women were going to Adult Literacy classes, seventeen others were trying to learn on their own, practising whatever they had learnt in the one or two years they had spent in school, while nine others were taking lessons from their husbands, children and employers.

Why was the level of education amongst women so dismally low? Among the petty bourgeoisie and the proletariat, a majority of the girls were withdrawn from school as soon as they reached puberty since they were considered grown-up enough to be 'married off'. Three out of the six girls from the petty bourgeoisie and proletarian sector were never sent to school due to poverty while the remaining had to stay at home because they were 'girls'. Among the subproletariat, never being sent to school or being withdrawn from school were all influenced by economic reasons. Withdrawal from school (or education) was necessary in order for the girls to join paid work directly or to help out with housework and sibling care while adults worked longer hours to make ends meet.

Debi who came from an informal petty bourgeoisie household and was withdrawn from school when she was twelve reminisced:

> 'Father said, "Girls, especially those from poor households (*gorib ghorer meyechchelera*), should not be seen outside too often after they become women. They become bad, they have bad thoughts and get into trouble." So the question of continuing school did not even arise'.

Halima, who was illiterate and came from a subproletarian household, felt that not sending her to school was a realistic choice on the part of her parents:

> 'I mean, what's the use? As mother used to say, "Ultimately you are going to end up stirring the pot. What good does education do for a girl in a poor household? Nothing!" And it's true. you know. I had to do the chores around the house, look after my younger siblings and do part-time domestic work since I was twelve. Now that I am married, I do the same things. Mother was right. Nothing changes for a girl'.

Apparently, adults in respondents' households of origin felt that returns from education are almost nil for girls since their prescribed social roles did not require educational achievement. This may have led to two types of behaviour on their part. In poorer subproletarian households, girls were either withdrawn from or not sent to school and they did paid work and housework, instead. In economically better-off petty bourgeoisie and proletarian households, a choice was made between education and marriage and/or respectability (expressed through sequestering a 'growing' girl) and, in both cases, the latter ideal got precedence. Overall, an ideology of 'domesticity', entailing a gamut of codes pertaining to restricted mobility, sexuality, honour and gender division of labour seems to be linked to the culmination of women's educational trajectories.

SOCIOECONOMIC AND HOUSEHOLD CHARACTERISTICS

By now it is clear that the women, who were interviewed, are largely homogeneous in their class locations in terms of household poverty status and living conditions. Arguably, since the sample contained respondents of varied regional and linguistic origin, a strictly 'cultural' analysis may be in order. I dwell mainly, however, on the socioeconomic domain since it defines the 'common' context in which the respondents' sexual and birth control trajectories take shape. The main trend in literacy, employment and wage patterns is more or less similar across religious groups, a commonality that is essential for exploration of the experience of a small defined sample. Any division on the basis of the various 'cultural' factors present in the sample will serve only to disintegrate the group without really revealing any substantial aggregate level trends. Further, while cultural determinants (relating to more 'ascribed' factors like ethnic origin, kinship patterns, marriage rituals) explain demographic behaviour in terms of child health and contraceptive use (e.g. Basu 1992), these do not really reveal how working class women carve out their day-to-day lives as active, though constrained agents.

I argue that given that there is a mix of first, second and third generation migrants among the women, and the fact that their length of stay in Calcutta varies between nine months and forty-three years, deciphering and establishing the influence of ascribed socio-cultural correlates on the basis of place of origin is next to impossible. Accordingly, I focus on religion as the only ascribed cultural factor in the analysis of birth control trajectories. Many Muslim women in the sample, irrespective of their socioeconomic status, said that they were prevented by religious decree to opt for sterilization. This factor seemed to make some obvious differences in the negotiations regarding birth control between Hindu and Muslim women in the sample.

Table 2.5 Wives' Work Status and Reasons for Not Doing Paid Work

Work Status	N	%
Currently engaged in paid work	59	(59)
Currently not engaged in paid work	41	(41)
Total	100	100
Reasons for not being in paid work		
Do not need	29.2	(12)
Prevented by husband, child-care, bad health	48.8	(20)
Prevented by lack of available jobs and pregnancy	22.0	(9)
Total	100.0	100

Table 2.5 gives the breakdown of the current work status of the women and reveals that although the majority (59%) does remunerative work, a large percentage (41%) does not. The growing majority of wage-earning women and the substantial minority of non-wage-earning women in the sample may be seen as representing the gradually changing matrix of female labour force participation in West Bengal. Indeed, need-based incentives for employment among women in the sample are also evident from the fact that of the 41 women who are not currently engaged in remunerative work (Table 2.5), a large number (48.8%) reported that they want to work but cannot because of ill health, excessive housework and child-care duties, lack of skill or, simply, husband's orders. Also, 22 percent reported being 'temporarily' out of work. These women were either pregnant at the time of the survey or had infants they needed to nurse. Some had quit work-

ing due to pregnancy and childbirth and could not find jobs when they wanted to go back to work. Women in this group felt that they would, however, go back to work as soon as they resolved child-care problems and more important, found a job. 'Give me a job—I'll do it,' said Nilima. 'If need be, I'll tie up my son on a leash, lock the door, keep his lunch and leave for work.'

In Table 2.6, which gives a breakdown of the types of occupation of respondents and their husbands, the term 'organized sector' refers to formal sector jobs with protected wages, social security benefits and access to unions. 'Unorganized sector' occupations are found in the informal economy and are characterized by casual, unprotected wages and absence of contractual relations with employer.

Occupation in the unorganized sector also includes self-employment as 'micro-entrepreneurs' (Tinker 1990:46). Weak market integration, low profit margins and strong face-to-face customer relations typically define self-employed enterprises in the unorganized sector.

The occupations elicited from the women are categorized as:

a. Factories/government services: jobs in large industrial manufacturing units in the public and private sector and in governmental offices as drivers, office personnel and similar capacities.

b. Small private business: employed as assistants in small grocery stores, catering services, decorating services and machine operators in small manufacturing units.

c. Skilled task-based service: task-based contracts for tailoring, construction work (like floor polishing, brick-laying, tile fixing), house painting, furniture-making, electrical wiring, bus driving, ticket collecting, rickshaw pulling (three wheeled 'cycle rickshaws' as they are known in India).

d. Self-Employment: includes street and door-to-door vending (grains, food, vegetables, toys, handkerchiefs, cloth pieces, lottery tickets, biscuits, canvas gloves, fish baits), paper bag making and selling, ironing, tutoring.

e. Domestic Services: employed as part time domestic help. Duties include washing utensils, clothes, sweeping and mopping floors, making tea, cooking, bringing children to and from school.

f. Home-based subcontracting: includes biri and papar rolling, assembling boxes and envelopes, pasting files and paper decorations, sewing gloves by hand.

g. Part home-based subcontracting-part domestic services: This includes occupations listed in (e) and (f).

h. Casual labour/Odd job: includes running errands, lifting loads, digging at construction sites.

i. Housework: includes all kinds of unpaid domestic work, including child-care at one's home.

Table 2.6 shows that despite the substantially high rate of labour force participation, women in the sample are all involved in the unorganized sector. This is typical of female labour force participation in the non-agricultural sector in India and Calcutta (Baud 1992: 76; N. Banerjee 1985: 23; Qadeer 1998). The breakdown of occupation categories reveals the highest concentration (41%) in housework. The majority of women in the sample engaged in remunerative work are employed as part-time domestic helpers (25%), a trend that typically reflects working class women's occupational formation in India (Basu and Sundar 1988:292). All occupations of income-earning women in the sample match with categories of occupations for women in Calcutta's unorganized sector (N. Banerjee 1985: 133-134).

Table 2.6 also indicates that trends in occupational concentration are not entirely similar across religious groups. While the second largest majority of Hindu women (34.8%) are in domestic services, the second largest group of Muslim women are engaged in home-based subcontracting which is done in one's room simultaneously with housework and child-care. Muslim women are perceived as being more 'restricted' than Hindu women whose occupational concentration reflects more contact with the public sphere. In fact, stricter literal observation of purdah in the Muslim community further underscores this notion.

From this data, however, we cannot deduce that it is religion per se which dictates the type of work done among the women. In fact, residence also seems to play a role in influencing occupational trends as discernible from Table 2.7. A majority of women in domestic services (51.2%) are concentrated in the southern part of the city. Slums surveyed in this area are located amid mostly middle and upper middle class residential neighborhoods (ibid.: 131). Those (40%) engaged in domestic outwork, on the other hand, are concentrated in the central part of the city which is mainly petty manufacturing and trading. So the type of dominant occupation in the areas may be a function of the socioeconomic characteristics of that area.

Table 2.6 Occupations of Wives and Husbands (%)

	Wife			Husband		
Organized Sector	Hindu	Muslim	Total (n)	Hindu	Muslim	Total (n)
Govt. Service / Factory (Wage)	-	-	-	9.1 (6)	-	6.0 (6)
Unorganised Sector						
Skilled task-based services (commission/ hourly and piece rate)	-	-	-	48.6 (32)	50.0 (17)	49.0 (49)
Small private business (wage)	-	-	-	12.1 (8)	14.7 (5)	13.0 (13)
Self-employed (profit)	16.7 (11)	11.8 (4)	15.0 (15)	12.1 (8)	35.3 (12)	20 (20)
Domestic labour and similar personal services (wage)	34.8 (23)	5.9 (2)	25.0 (25)	-	-	-
Home-based subcontracting (piece rate)	4.5 (3)	23.5 (8)	11.0 (11)	-	-	-
Part-domestic/ part-sub-contracting (wage/ piece rate)	7.6 (5)	8.8 (3)	8.0 (8)	-	-	-
Casual labour/ Odd job (hourly rate/ commission)	-	-	-	15.1 (10)	-	10.0 (10)
Non-remunerative work Housework (including child-care) only	36.4 (24)	50.0 (17)	41 (41)	-	-	-
Other No occupation	-	-	-	3.0 (2)	-	2.0 (2)
Total (n)	100.0 (66)	100.0 (34)	100.0 (100)			

Table 2.7 Type of Work of Wives, Area-wise

	Domestic Services	Self Employment	Home-based Subcontracting	Part Domestic-part Subcontracting	House-work only	Total (n)
North	7.7 (2)	30.8 (8)	3.9 (1)	11.4 (3)	46.2 (12)	100.0 (26)
Central	5.0 (1)	-	40.0 (8)	15.0 (3)	40.0 (8)	100.0 (20)
East	7.7 (1)	15.4 (2)	-	-	76.9 (10)	100.0 (13)
South	51.2 (21)	12.2 (5)	4.9 (2)	4.9 (2)	26.8 (11)	100.0 (41)

With regard to work status of husbands, Table 2.6 shows that only two of the respondents openly admitted that their husbands have no occupations. Further probing revealed that these two husbands were out of work for more than five months. The probing also revealed that among others, husbands of fourteen women had been out of work for the past one week to four months. The latter group of women felt that their husbands were only temporarily out of work and hoped that they would resume working in the near future. Thus, when asked about specific occupations of husbands, all except the two women mentioned earlier reported some form of employment for husbands. This tendency to make sure to report husband's occupation is in sharp contrast to some women's declaration of their own earnings. During the interviews, these women said they had no jobs besides the domestic obligations in their own homes. Then, while describing their daily routines, they mentioned making paper bags or rolling biris, which further probing revealed were a source of much needed income for the household. I also found women reporting themselves as 'housewives' helping their husbands and marital kin at work, essentially as unpaid family labor. Their contribution to household income of course remained undocumented. This trait is typical of women's work experience in India. Chapters 4 and 5 will show how this pervading ideology, venerating women's 'place at home as wife and mother' and the husband's role as 'breadwinner' even though the reality is very different, have far reaching implications in terms of gender construction and reconstruction in sexual and birth control experiences. In this book, these women are described as they perceive themselves: unpaid home-makers.

Table 2.6 also shows that 49 percent of the husbands are clumped in the skilled-task based employment category followed by 20 percent who are self-employed in small private businesses. This trend roughly continues across religious groups where the majority of both Hindu and Muslim husbands fall in the skilled task-based employment category. However, while the second largest percentage among Muslim husbands is self-employed (35.3%), Hindu husbands are almost evenly distributed across self-employment (12.1%), wage work in small private business (12.1%) and casual labourer/odd job (15.1%) groups.

Table 2.8 : Monthly Income of Husbands and Wives (in rupees)

	Wife			Husband		
	Hindu	Muslim	Total (n)	Hindu	Muslim	Total (n)
0	36.4 (24)	50.0 (17)	41 (41)	18.2 (6)	5.9 (8)	14 (14)
20-99	10.6 (7)	11.8 (4)	11 (11)	-	-	-
100-199	6.1 (4)	20.6 (7)	11 (11)	1.5 (1)	-	1 (1)
200-299	13.6 (9)	11.8 (4)	13 (13)	3.0 (2)	2.9 (1)	3 (3)
300-399	27.3 (18)	2.9 (1)	19 (19)	9.1 (6)	2.9 (1)	7 (7)
400-599	4.5 (3)	2.9 (1)	4 (4)	9.1 (6)	23.5 (8)	14 (14)
600-799	1.5 (1)	-	1 (1)	16.7 (11)	20.6 (7)	18 (18)
800-999	-	-	-	9.1 (6)	8.8 (3)	9 (9)
1000-1500	-	-	-	10.6 (7)	23.5 (8)	15 (15)
1500+	-	-	-	4.5 (3)	-	3 (3)
Don't Know	-	-	-	18.2 (12)	-	16 (16)
Total (n)	100.0 (100)	100.0 (100)	100.0 (100)	100.0 (100)	100.0 (100)	100.0 (100)

Table 2.8, on monthly income, clearly elucidates the gender differentials in remuneration, an understandable outcome of the differential nature and variety of employment opportunities available to the husbands versus wives in the sample. These

findings also reflect women's employment trends in India (Baud 1992; N. Banerjee 1985). Income patterns across religion are somewhat dissimilar in that after housework, which provides zero income, most Hindu women are concentrated in the Rs.300–Rs.399 monthly wage group followed by the Rs.200–Rs. 299 range. Although the largest percentage (50%) of Muslim wives are also in housework like the Hindu group, the largest concentration among wives engaged in remunerative work is in the Rs.100–Rs.199 group followed by the Rs.200–Rs.299 group. Perhaps, then, because they concentrate on specific jobs, Muslim women tend to earn less than Hindu women in the sample.

Table 2.8 also shows that according to the reports of wives, Muslim husbands are somewhat more concentrated in higher income categories compared to Hindu husbands. This finding should be interpreted with some caution. We have seen earlier that more Muslim husbands were Calcutta-born (implying second or third generation migrants) than Hindu husbands. Hindu husbands are more likely to be first generation migrants and hence, relatively new in the city, new in their jobs (therefore, earning lower wages) and still looking for more lucrative avenues of employment. In any case, incomes in the unorganized sector fluctuate and there is no certainty that individuals' incomes will remain stable or increase/decrease with time. Capturing these fluid income situations is difficult in a cross-sectional survey such as the one on which the present study is based. Therefore, the relatively higher current incomes of Muslim husbands should not automatically lead one to believe that on an absolute level, Muslim husbands are economically more stable and better off than their Hindu counterparts, or that Muslim wives' lower contributions is a function of the higher earnings of their husbands. Overall, the foregoing descriptions reveal the impoverished working class characteristics and the precarious economic condition of the average household in the sample.

FERTILITY-BASED CHARACTERISTICS

Mean age at marriage for women in urban West Bengal is 17.4 (Census of India, 1991 in Occasional Paper of 1988), which contrasts only slightly with that of the sample: 16.9 among Hindus and 16.3 among Muslims (Table 2.9).

Table 2.9 Age at Marriage and Fertility History by Religion

	Hindu	Muslim
Mean Age at Marriage	16.9	16.3
Mean Number of Pregnancies	3.4	5.3
Mean Number of Children Ever Born	2.9	4.7
Mean Number of Living Children	2.6	4.2
Total (n)	(66)	(34)

Figures for the mean age at marriage quoted in the Census of 1991 show this to be 27.4 years, which deviates widely from previous reporting. One cannot rule out the possibility of a radical shift in marriage customs in urban West Bengal, though it seems more likely that the change is due to differing measurement and/or reporting parameters in the 1991 Census (GOI 1991). The average number of pregnancies is higher for Muslim women (see Table 2.9). Meanwhile, the Total Fertility Rate (TFR) in urban India is 3.2 (*Health on the March*, 1996-97). Since TFR is a projection including women of all childbearing ages, it is not directly comparable to women of all age groups found in the sample. But on comparing the TFR to that of women (n=10) in their late childbearing years (40-49), I found that the average varied between 5 and 5.8 for the whole sample and between 4.8 and 5.5. for both Hindus and Muslims. Thus, both groups in the sample seem to have higher than average fertility rates. Overall, religion does not seem to make any difference to the nature of the sample. Some fertility related differences, however, are noticeable. Accordingly, the birth control experiences of Hindu and Muslim women are analysed separately for comparison. Extant research asserts that variations in intra-household division of labour and allocation of resources need to be analysed in relation to a household's position in the development cycle (Beneria and Roldan 1987; Baud 1992). In the study sample, 86 percent of the households roughly fall in the 'early' phase while 14 percent are located in the 'advanced' phase (Table 2.10). Presumably, compared to the advanced phase, women in the early phase are in a more vulnerable situation. During this time, more pregnancies occur and, consequently, there are more child-care responsibilities. There are also more mouths to feed with less money as children make either no or relatively little economic contribution. The period is also marked by less household autonomy for women due to existing age hierarchies in the household.

Thus, the various characteristics just described further corroborate the 'typical Calcutta working class character' of the study sample. Having established the characteristics that make the sample a cohesive one, we can now turn to an exploration of its intricate differences.

Table 2.10 Households : Family Life Cycle, Family Structure and Mean Age of Spouses

	Family Type		
Early Phase	Nuclear	Extended	Total
1. Couple without children	(2)	(4)	6
Average Age of Wife	22	20	
Average Age of Husband	23	24	
2. Couple with children under 7	(7)	(12)	19
Average Age of Wife	23	22	
Average Age of Husband	30	29	
3. Couple with female children between 7-18 and male between 7-21 and children under 7	(21)	(19)	40
Average Age of Wife	30	28	
Average Age of Husband	42	38	
4. Couple with female children between 7-18 and male between 7-21 and no children under 7	(13)	(8)	21
Average Age of Wife	34	31	
Average Age of Husband	45	40	
Advanced Phase			
5. Couple with 18+ female children and 21+ male children and children under 7	(5)	-	5
Average Age of Wife	38	-	
Average Age of Husband	52	-	
6. Couple with 18+ female children and 21+ male children and no children under 7	(6)	(3)	9
Average Age of Wife	42	36	
Average Age of Husband	50	43	
Total (n) = 100			

NOTES

1. CMDA 1991
2. In this study a household is typically defined as a unit in which a group of people live while sharing a budget. A family, on the other hand, refers to a unit where all the members of the household have kin-based relations.
3. A girl child may live at her natal home until puberty even though she may be married off at a young age. The beginning of puberty is marked by the gauna ceremony. After the gauna, the young bride leaves home for her marital household which effectively starts her sexual relationship with her husband. Demographers consider gauna a proximate determinant of fertility in South Asia (Basu 1992).

3

A PLACE CALLED HOME
MARITAL ALLOCATION OF RESOURCES AND EXCHANGE PATTERNS

In order to explore the material and ideological contexts and their articulation in terms of household exchanges in women's current marital households, I focus on two areas of household exchange: (*a*) women's monetary contribution to household expenses in relation to their husbands and the ensuing dynamics of differential conjugal autonomy; and (*b*) the related dynamics of gender division of labour within the household.

HUSBANDS AND WIVES AS EARNERS

The dynamics of resource contribution by spouses within households revealed that notwithstanding the necessity of women's paid work in poor households, all positions in the higher category of proletarians belong to the husbands. The location in a more stable sector may not necessarily correspond to higher cash acquisition particularly in the skilled task-based service group but chances of mobility and quicker increases in income are always greater than in domestic services and home-based subcontracting, where the wives are concentrated (Table 3.1). Also, between the income-earning spouses in the sample, husbands always earn more.

Table 3.1 : Distribution of Husbands and Wives by Current Occupation (%)

	Wife	Husband
Proletariat	-	6.0 (6)
Sub-proletariat		
General waged	1.0 (1)	13.0 (13)
Skilled-task based services	-	49.0 (49)
Autonomous services	15.0 (15)	20.0 (20)
Personal services	25.0 (25)	-
Home-based subcontracting	11.0 (11)	-
Part personal service-part subcontracting	7.0 (7)	-
Casual / Seasonal services	-	10.0 (10)
Others	41.0 (41)	2.0 (2)
Total (n)	100.0 (100)	100.0 (100)

In the context of exploring women's articulations as active (although constrained) agents in sexual and birth control negotiations (Chapters 4 and 5), it is useful to see how women exercise agency in arranging the material basis of their daily lives. This entails decomposition of the respondents' households and revelation of some of their internal hierarchies. 'Household' is a common space where individuals live together under one roof and share a budget. In this book, all households are based on kinship relationships. Women enter their nuclear or extended marital households, each carrying her individual baggage of class and gender history. How do the educational and income differences between husband and wife manifest themselves in household resource allocations and exchanges? How much control, if any, do women have over these exchanges? How do women view their lives in the household situation that they are in? These are some of the issues explored in the following section. Because of the centrality of husband-wife interactions in matters related to sex and birth control, I focus on interactions within the conjugal unit. References to variations between nuclear and extended households are made when pertinent.

Based on the types of occupation of family members, money enters the household either daily, weekly or monthly. I compute all amounts on a monthly basis largely because respondents mostly refer to household expenses in terms of a month. Also, rent, and in some cases, electricity bills, food item bills and children's school fees are paid monthly (the latter in very few cases since most children who went to school had free schooling). Charges for books and writing materials are paid annually. Two patterns of household income allocation, emerge for women in the sample. The 'pooling' pattern involves a situation where both husband and wife contribute to the common family fund for household expenses, while the housekeeping allowance set includes those wives who do not earn at all or those who keep their incomes as 'pin-money' or save their earnings, while their husbands provide household expenses. What follows is a description of distribution of wives within pooling continuum and housekeeping allowance sets. Since husbands and wives in three households reported no income at the time of the survey, they are dropped from this part of the analysis. Five types of households emerged:

GROUP A

Wives who contribute a notable amount of the monthly pool (more than 40%) and whose husbands pool and are more or less regular providers (six of the 97 wives in the sample).

GROUP B

Wives who contribute more than 40 percent of the monthly pool but whose husbands have almost stopped contributing, or do so irregularly, reasons ranging from illness to unwillingness to work, alcoholism to just plain unemployment (22 of the 97 wives). Half of the husbands in this group had no income whatsoever.

GROUP C

Wives who contribute less than 40 percent of the monthly pool and whose husbands pool and remain the main economic providers (26 of 97 wives).

Subsamples in the housekeeping allowance set include :

GROUP D

Wives receiving allowance from husbands (and sometimes other members of kin groups), while their earnings are used as savings or pin-money (five of 97).

GROUP E

Wives receiving allowances only, not earning any income (38 out of 97).

How do the women's lives vary within and across these groups? A more detailed look at elements of control over household income,[1] family decisions,[2] husbands' participation in housework,[3] husbands' drinking[4] and beating,[5] and women's feelings about their lives[6] will help us to get a better profile of these women and of the nature of this 'place called home.' Incidentally, with reference to husband's participation in housework, even among husbands who help, the 'type' of work done is limited and almost exclusively concentrated in activities outside the home: carrying out formal transactions, going to the shop, repairing roofs, 'holding' infants while chatting and playing cards as the wife cooked dinner. Other more domestic activities like cooking or fetching water were done on 'demand': for instance, when the wife was ill or had to do remunerative work; or when there was no grown-up daughter or female kin present to perform the task.

GROUP A

Despite being a small group of only six households, some unique features of wives' interaction and control emerge. The wives are evenly spread across domestic, autonomous and part-domestic-part home-based subcontracting services, while the husbands are concentrated in the lowest wage categories of the skilled task-based service subproletariat group. Thus, although husbands invariably earn more than wives, differences between earnings of husbands and wives are small. All the women spend their entire earnings on household expenses. Husbands, on the other hand exercise more control over their own incomes. Three of the six husbands put all of their income into the pool but take money from it for regular personal spending (transport, biri, cigarette, tea, paan). Two husbands contribute a fixed amount to the pool and keep the remainder for personal expenses. Only one husband, keeps all his money to himself and gives it to his wife when she asks for it. Despite the relative control over income exercised by husbands, wives have full knowledge of their family incomes and exact earnings of their husbands. Four husbands (66.7%) help with housework frequently or sometimes. Five husbands (83.3%) seem to be more accountable and responsible in that they take an interest in making family decisions with their wives. Moreover, most husbands neither drink (66.7%) nor beat (83.3%) their wives. Naturally, this was a major source of relief for the wives. They felt they were 'lucky' that their 'men are good'. The wives' main worries centred around material and health aspects, underscored by some hope to see things through to the end, mostly with the husbands.

GROUP B

The 22 households in this group have some of the most conflictual relations. Emergence of 'female headed households', where the husband is actually present but not the main economic provider, appears to create clashing values, feelings of guilt and sometimes, extreme frustration on the part of wives and the propensity to exert excessive control and to abandon the family, on the part of husbands. Since wives' adoption of a traditionally male role occurs more out of need than choice, conjugal interaction may be characterized by friction and stress for wives. The situation becomes more complex for wives who make concerted efforts to somehow 'live up' to their 'normative' societal roles while the material realities of their lives and behaviour of their husbands make the exercise largely impossible and costly in terms of health and well-being.

Sarju, age 25, is a case in point. Her 'young nuclear' household is one of the poorest in the sample. She lives with a husband, twenty years her senior, and their nine-month-old daughter who survived after a series of miscarriages. Her husband, a bricklayer in the skilled task-based service sector, always worked irregularly because of his health and over the past month had stopped working completely. As a result, Sarju became the main earner of the household. She works in four houses as a part-time domestic servant. Besides running home in between jobs to nurse her daughter who is looked after by the female kin living next door, she does not have much time to buy daily provisions or even to cook. Hence, most of the time her husband does the cooking and goes to the bazar with money that Sarju gives him. Sarju knows that every day, her husband drinks away some of the money she gives him for the bazar. She has quarrelled with him and 'created many scenes' about this. At the same time, she does not want to pursue the issue too often, because after all, the husband is an elder and it must be very humiliating for him to drink out of his wife's money, in the first place. Sarju goes to sleep every night at 1 a.m. after washing the lunch and dinner utensils. This, despite the fact that she has to get up to nurse her daughter and go to work by 9 a.m. She does not 'allow' her husband to do the utensils because cooking food is one thing but washing the 'dirty' dishes is another. According to Sarju, 'that is a woman's job'.

Fifteen (68.2%) of the wives in this group were like Sarju, working as part-time domestics with a frenetic routine both at home and outside the home. Another four complemented part-time domestic work with home-based subcontracting work, while the remaining three made a living in the autonomous subproletariat sector making and selling paper bags. As mentioned earlier, 11 of the husbands (50%) were not earning any income over the past four months. Two of these, who belonged to the proletariat, had been laid off after receiving a small benefit package from the jute and chemical factories in which they worked. One also belonged to the general waged subproletariat, while the remaining eight were in task-based services. At the time of the interview they were, to a large extent, 'dependent' upon their wives for survival. Propensity to control and demand among these husbands may be seen in this context as an attempt to gain back the importance they may have felt their incomes gave them in the past.

Of the husbands who earned an income, employment was spread across the skilled task-based service sector and that of casual labourers in temporary jobs. Six of these husbands (over a quarter of the total) kept their money to themselves and exercised discretion in giving it to their wives. In fact, a number of the wives did not know how much their husbands earned. In contrast, husbands who did not earn were mostly given open access to the common fund although, over-reaching 'limits' on the part of husbands and consequently wives' complaints led to quarrels and beatings. All these women spend their entire monthly earnings on the household. Also, 14 of the wives (63.6%) made critical family decisions on their own. This cannot be interpreted entirely as 'control' since wives said they did it 'because husbands do not care'. Taking family decisions on one's own then, may be seen as a duty in the absence of other options. This becomes more evident with the knowledge that half of the husbands made no effort to help in household work and a majority, 18 (81.8%) of them, either drank every day or as soon as they could get their hands on some money (be it their own or their wives', as in Sarju's case). Thirteen husbands (59.1%) also beat their wives. In this milieu wives felt they had to struggle very hard with their responsibilities, efforts to earn money and perform their domestic obligations.

Consequently, while a majority (59.2%) expressed that their major concern in life was to make both ends meet and manage the material domain, the remaining nine (40.9%) expressed mental agonies and frustrations wrought by husbands and marital kin.

GROUP C

The 26 husbands in this group fell in the median income group, working mostly as members of the subproletariat in skilled task-based and autonomous services. Six (23.1%) of them kept some and nine (34.6%) kept all of their incomes to themselves. In contrast, all the wives—employed in domestic outwork, autonomous and domestic services—spent their entire income on the family. Three of the wives (11.4%) did not have any idea about their monthly family income, while four (15.4%) were ignorant of the quantity of their husbands' incomes.

Fifteen men, or more than half of the husbands, did not help with any housework. With regard to family decisions, nine husbands (34.6%) exercised ultimate veto power while another nine took joint decisions with wives. Half the wives reported being beaten and seven wives (a little more than a quarter) said their husbands drank alcohol when they had money. Of the 26 wives, 16 (61.6%) reported that their major worries in life revolved around meeting basic survival needs: getting enough for children to eat, worrying about girls' weddings and boys' education, getting a bigger, better place to live, maintaining good health and so on. The remaining 10 (38.4%), expressed a sense of hopelessness about their lives and discontent about their relationships with their husbands and, sometimes, with their marital kin.

GROUP D

For wives in the housekeeping allowance set, the better economic positions of husbands and the absence or marginality of paid work for wives created somewhat different expectations and reciprocities in conjugal interactions. Three out of the five wives in Group D maintained that their husbands gave their total incomes as allowance, and used money from it whenever they wanted. Four out of five husbands in this group were concentrated in the higher wage and relatively stable subproletariat sectors of general waged and skilled task-based services. Wives, on the other hand, engaged in rolling biri (home-based subproletariat work) and making paper bags (autonomous services), two of the lowest paid and unstable occupations in the subproletariat sector. These wives used their own earned money to buy clothes and books for children when required or saved to make jewellery for children's weddings. Four of these wives said that during 'these troubled times' they owed their economic support to their husbands. On the housework front, three of the husbands helped with fetching water or vegetables from the market when their wives (or daughter/s) could not find time to do these chores. The remaining two did not help with housework. One woman in this subsample did not know what the family income was while another had no idea how much her husband earned. Again, in four out of five cases, wives felt that it was mostly their duty to make all the family decisions, in terms of cooking food, buying clothes, asking children to study because this was seen as part of 'a wife's and mother's job' and 'men would not know what to do'. Ultimately, however, things had to work according to the husband's wishes ('If before leaving, he says, "I want kabab for dinner today", I will have to make the necessary arrangements. I will have rice and dal with my girls. But it will be kabab for him all right!'). Failure to do so often resulted in quarrelling and beating as the report of regular beating by three out of five wives in this subsample made apparent. Additionally, all husbands drank regularly either on pay days or every day, and it was not for the wives to decide whether they should or should not: 'It's my money; I shall do what I want with it.' Regarding worries in life, four out of the five wives reported concern for material well-being. Surprisingly (in contrast to the frustration expressed by some of the wives in the pooling group) the high incidence of wife-beating did not feature as a major worry among the women in this subsample of the housekeeping allowance group. In fact, a typical response among the three wives who were regularly beaten by their husbands was, 'This is what my life is going to be, this is my fate, what is the use of complaining?' We will see how this relative passivity influences the sexual and birth control negotiations of these women.

GROUP E

The economic stability of these thirty-eight households is greater than most of the others in the sample. All the four working proletariat husbands belonged here, along with the highest concentration of general waged subproletariat (61.5%, that is eight out of 13 husbands in the entire sample) and higher wage skilled task-based subproletariat (17 husbands). As mentioned earlier, wives in this group do not earn any income. Interestingly, nine (69.2%) of the 13 women in income-earning households who could not give even a rough estimate of their family incomes, belonged to this group. Also, of the 16 women who did not know their husbands' incomes, the highest concentration (7) were in this subgroup. Half of the wives reported that their husbands kept some or all of their incomes to themselves. The other half maintained that their husbands gave all their incomes to the family fund and took money from it when they wanted. The high degree of control over income exercised by husbands was typically regarded by some of these wives as 'normal' as the act fell into men's prescribed role domain ('He should keep the money. He is a man, he will know what to do. I am stupid, I won't be able to take care of the money'). Consequently, as many as 16 wives reported that their husbands had ultimate veto power on family decisions and the 14, who asserted that they (the wives) took family decisions justified this seeming paradox with a preconceived gender differentiation: 'husbands being men, cannot cope with family decisions'. For all these wives, the normative role was in making the majority of family decisions: what to cook, when to clean the house, when to wash clothes, when to ask children to study. Thus, typically, most husbands—23 of 38 (60.5%)—did not help with housework while 7 (21.2%) helped only when the wives were ill, or preoccupied with other housework. Instances of husbands drinking and regularly beating wives were relatively low in this group. Only 14 wives (36.8%) reported that their husbands drank alcohol either every day or on pay days and 'special occasions', while the majority—24—did not drink at all. A similar pattern emerged in responses to questions about beating. Only 10 wives (26.3%) talked about regular beatings by husbands.

I found eliciting responses from the wives in Group E about beating and alcoholism more difficult than in any other group. Most of the time wives averted their eyes or just nodded their heads while responding and their uneasiness and reluctance to answer my rather pointed questions was obvious. This may be partly because these wives were entirely dependent upon their husbands' financial input for survival and were, therefore, scared to portray their husbands negatively. Also, since the households in this subsample belonged to relatively 'higher' social classes, norms of respectability and honour presumably carried more weight. Consequently, admitting to 'lower class' practices like abuse and alcoholism might perhaps, in their eyes, jeopardize their class positions. Thus, with regard to view of life, the majority (63.2%) expressed concern about their material needs and children's well-being. Of the remainder, seven believed that they had to accept what fate had in store for them.

Let us now turn to examine some aspects of domestic work exchanges in the pooling continuum (Groups A, B and C) and the housekeeping allowance set (Groups D and E) according to the phase in the family life-cycle and kinship structure of households. Households in the 'Early Phase' are referred to as 'young nuclear/extended' and those in the 'Advanced Phase' are referred to as 'adult nuclear/extended'. There were only three adult extended households in the sample; consequently, they were dropped from the analysis. Differences between the groups is emphasized in this section.

HOUSEHOLDS IN THE EARLIER PHASES OF THE FAMILY CYCLE

Table 3.2 shows that in the young nuclear households, average hours worked per week were greater for women in the pooling than for the women in the housekeeping allowances sets. The reverse happens when these hours are broken down into segments dedicated to paid work and housework. Thus, women not engaged in paid work (Group E) dedicated more time to housework than any other group (85.1 hours) followed by those in Group D (70 hours). The internal distribution across groups indicates that for wives in Group A, economic need necessitates longer hours of paid work and relative neglect of housework. The remaining working wives in the pooling and housekeeping allowance sets (Groups B, C and D), however, have to take care of domestic obligations before engaging in paid work. The situation is most arduous for wives Groups B and C, who needed to strike a mean between paid work and unpaid domestic work, resulting in the sacrifice of outings and leisure activities in order for these wives to attain their objectives.[7] Since all women in this group are in the young nuclear cycle, relatively more child-care duties and absence of regular help from school-going children, result in long total work days. This raises the issue of help received by wives in domestic work.

Table 3.3 gives a comparative distribution of help received by women from other family members within the household. Note that kin and children helping the wife in her domestic work are regular helpers in all cases, whereas all husbands who participate in housework, however, are not. Therefore, only husbands who help with housework frequently are compared to these kin and children. Moreover, help from husbands who help only 'sometimes' is contingent upon their moods and any unique situations arising in the households. Overall, it would be unfair to compare their contributions with that of mostly, daughter and female kin who make time to engage in domestic tasks more regularly in the women's household.

Table 3.2 Women's Mean Weekly Working Hours by Household Income Allocation Groups* A, B, C

	Group A Wifes contribute > 40% Husband stable provider			Group B Wife contributes > 40% Husband unstable provider			Group C Wife contributes < 40% Husband stable provider		
Phase of Family Cycle	Unpaid Domestic Work	Paid Work	Total	Unpaid Domestic Work	Paid Work	Total	Unpaid Domestic Work	Paid Work	Total
Young Nuclear (n=42)	49.0	80.5	129.5	65.1	49.7	114.8	69.5	45.7	115.2
Young Extended (n=41)	60.7	63.0	123.7	56.0	67.4	123.4	63.8	38.9	102.7
Adult Nuclear (n=11)	56.0	70.0	126.0	60.7	51.3	112.0	49.0	63.0	112.0

Table 3.2 (cont.) Women's Mean Weekly Working Hours by Household Income Allocation Groups* D, E

	Group D Wife's money not used for household expenses Husband gives allowance			Group E Wife does not earn Husband gives allowance		
Phase of Family Cycle	Unpaid Domestic Work	Paid Work	Total	Unpaid Domestic Work	Paid Work	Total
Young Nuclear (n=42)	70.0	38.5	108.5	85.1	-	85.1
Young Extended (n=41)	80.0	21.0	101.0	91.4	-	91.4
Adult Nuclear (n=11)	56.0	42.0	98.0	78.2	-	78.2

* Note : Extended household in advance phases have been dropped due to small number of cases in each group.

As Table 3.3 shows, female kin and daughters help much more than sons. I found that it was very common for daughters to come back from school in the afternoon and cook the rice or chop vegetables. No such responsibilities were accorded to sons. In fact, both in nuclear and extended households, women took help from young sisters, mothers, mothers-in-law, the distant female relative next door in matters related to cooking, washing, baby-sitting and so on, much more than they did from male relatives. The extent and nature of help taken, however, varied with women's locations in the phases of the family cycle.

In the young extended households (Table 3.2), trends in the total work hours across groups are similar to those in the young nuclear cycle (i.e., wives in Groups A and B) compared to wives in the housekeeping allowances sets (Groups D and E) while those in Group C occupy an intermediate position. Looking at internal distribution within these groups, however, one discovers that only wives in the neediest households (Groups A and B) put in more hours of remunerated work than housework. For wives in Groups C, D and E, once again domestic obligations come first. An interesting variation occurs when women in the young extended cycle are compared to wives in the young nuclear cycle in the same groups. For those in Group C in extended households, hours of housework are less than for those in nuclear households. The trend reverses for wives in the housekeeping allowances sets (Groups D and E) in extended households who do 10 and 6.3 more hours of work respectively than their counterparts in the nuclear households. The reason for the difference lies in the varied economic situations and kinship compositions of the households. Women in the extended households live along with their marital kin (in 87% of the cases) so the 'young' wives in these households are bound to their domestic domain not only as mother, wife and housewife, but also as daughter-in-law. This is one of the most vulnerable roles endured by women in Indian society, placing upon them a host of duties and obligations. In this instance, the internal age hierarchy in the household also makes it very difficult for a woman to escape from these duties.

With this in view, a high percentage (87.8%) of wives in Group C solicit help from female kin and this is essential for the survival of these extended households (this is not possible, of course, for wives in nuclear families whose female kin do not live with them and for whom help comes only with visits from mothers, sisters or mothers-in-law). The situation was different for young extended households in the housekeeping allowances sets, where the wives' monetary contribution was less significant. These wives were expected to do a phenomenal amount of domestic work (80 hours/week for those in Group D and 91.4 hours/week for those in Group E) which exceeded the hours spent in housework and child care by wives across the entire sample (Table 3.2). Thus, even while counting on help from resident female kin seems to be fundamental to the housework strategies of wives in the young extended households (Table 3.2) a wife's contribution to household expenses seems to make a difference in the quality of help received.

HOUSEHOLDS IN THE ADVANCED PHASE OF THE LIFE CYCLE

For nuclear households in the Advanced Phase, the total number of weekly work hours of wives decreases in comparison to those in the nuclear phase (Table 3.2). Wives tend to reduce their pace of work slowly, adjusting between paid work and housework according to the immediate necessities of their situations, current conjugal dynamics and available assistance. However, it is very difficult to make any generalizations here since the eleven women in this group are spread across the different income allocation groups. Additionally, I only consider those who received help from older children, female kin and husbands. Consequently, the cases vary between one to three in each of the categories. The findings therefore, should be considered as pertaining to cases instead of groups.

The circumstances of the wives in the adult nuclear phase were somewhat different from the young nuclear group in several ways. First, there were more adult children in the household to contribute money to the household pool. Second, presence of older children, especially daughter/s, largely mitigated domestic demands on wives. On the whole, therefore, these wives were able to relax more, sleep for a while after lunch or work in one house (instead of three or four) as domestic helpers, cut down hours of home-based subcontracting work and, generally, try to regain their health and energy.

Interestingly, wives in Group A in the adult phase do an average 10.5 hours less paid work than their counterparts in the young nuclear households (Table 3.2). Most likely, coming from the

Table 3.3 Husbands, Daughters, Sons and Other Female Kin Who Help in Domestic Work by Income Allocation Groups, A, B and C Phase of Family Cycle (%)

	Group A Wife contributes > 40% Husband stable provider				Group B Wife contributes > 40% Husband unstable provider				Group C Wife contributes < 40% Husband stable provider			
Phase of Family Cycle	Husband (s)	Daughter (s)	Son (s)	Other Female Kin	Husband (s)	Daughter (s)	Son (s)	Other Female Kin	Husband (s)	Daughter (s)	Son (s)	Other Female Kin
Young Nuclear (n=42)	50 (n=1)	-	-	100 (n=1)	20 (n=2)	16.7 (n=1)	-	83.3 (n=5)	1.3.3 (n=2)	80 (n=8)	-	20 (n=2)
Young Extended (n=41)	-	33.3 (n=1)	-	66.7 (n=2)	37.5 (n=3)	14.2 (n=1)	-	75 (n=6)	33.3 (n=3)	12.5 (n=1)	-	87.8 (n=7)
Adult Nuclear (n=11)	100 (n=1)	-	-	100 (n=1)	33.3 (n=1)	33.3 (n=1)	33.3 (n=1)	33.3 (n=1)	100 (n=1)	100 (n=1)	-	-

Table 3.3 (contd.) Husbands, Daughters, Sons and Other Female Kin Who Help in Domestic Work by Income Allocation Groups, D and E Phase of Family Cycle (%)

	Group D Wife's money not used for household expenses Husband gives allowance				Group E Wife does not earn Husband gives allowance			
Phase of Family Cycle	Husband (s)	Daughter (s)	Son (s)	Other Female Kin	Husband (s)	Daughter (s)	Son (s)	Other Female Kin
Young Nuclear (n=42)	50 (n=1)	-	-	-	30.8 (n=4)	50 (n=4)	-	50 (n=4)
Young Extended (n=41)	-	100 (n=1)	-	-	10 (n=2)	53.8 (n=7)	-	46.2 (n=6)
Adult Nuclear (n=11)	-	100 (n=1)	-	-	40 (n=2)	60 (n=3)	-	-

neediest households, these wives had very rigorous paid work schedules in the younger phase of their life-cycles. Now, with relative economic stability of older income-earning children and older husbands, they could afford to slow down. Barring Group A, the opposite tendency appears when older wives in the nuclear households are compared to their younger counterparts in the remaining pooling and housekeeping allowances groups (Groups B, C, D and E). Recall that these wives in the young nuclear group had to take care of domestic obligations first (and only domestic obligations in case of Group E) before dedicating time to remunerative work. During this time, a lower percentage of wives can elicit help from daughters and husbands as compared to those in the adult nuclear cycle (Table 3.3). As the situation changes with availability of daughters and constancy of older husbands (in Groups A and C) in the adult nuclear cycle to help with housework, income-earning wives in Groups B, C and D seem to take advantage of this help and try and earn some more, as much as their reduced energy and health allows. In the long run, therefore, their total number of work hours cannot exceed that of the young nuclear wives. Similarly, wives in Group E decrease their domestic duties as they grow older (Table 3.2) and more household work duties are vested on daughter/s (Table 3.3).

How then do the life experiences of women, beginning from their childhood to their marital years unfold? What strategies are they able to devise to balance their paid and unpaid work? What implications do these experiences have in terms of class and gender reproduction at the societal level?

Exploration of experiences in the women's childhoods show that their gender-based socialization through. education, housework, child care and paid work are set at an early age and these influence their decisions throughout life. For instance, in terms of paid work, women (if they are employed) are placed in relatively less secure and less stable occupations than their husbands. Patterns of income allocation and control that emerge show, that among households in the sample, husbands: (*a*) keep some money for personal expenses before contributing to the pool; or (*b*) keep all money to themselves and contribute (if they so desire) as and when asked by wives; or (*c*) contribute their entire income as part of the pool or as allowances, but draw money from this contribution every time they need to buy biris or cigarettes, cups of tea, paan or alcohol. In all three modes, women's socialization makes them naturally accept that husbands have access and control over their own (and, in some cases, their wives') incomes. Thus, much of women's articulation of rights, duties and goals occurs while they define and redefine their gender spheres, drawing from the past, evaluating the present and their current conjugal experiences.

In terms of the linkage between women's ability to command agency in the household and their paid work, it may be said that at an absolute level, paid work is exhaustive and back-breaking, wages and incomes are low and women's control over their own earnings gives them only limited options to negotiate their share in unpaid domestic work. However, contribution to the common family fund helps women to look after the collective well-being of their families, especially their children. In fact, in Group A, more husbands and wives are able to make joint family decisions, as opposed to some of the other groups, where the wife makes her decision alone or the decision of the husband dominates. Also, more women engaged in paid work are able to articulate their needs and frustrations about their husbands.

No doubt, these women's circles of influence are very restricted. Their negotiating capacity is confined to resolving whether to focus on paid work or unpaid domestic work or to decrease their share of domestic work by having other female kin or daughters fill in for them. Where husbands help in the housework, the actual tasks performed are confined to activities outside the house (e.g., shopping) rather than inside (e.g., cooking, cleaning, washing). Thus, most women are not able to decrease their share of household tasks by having husbands assume them. Additionally, pocket money for the husband to drink on pay days and to buy cigarettes, biris, tea and paan are withdrawn from the common family fund while the wife may be sacrificing her own well-being (skipping lunch, eating less, wearing the same torn clothes year after year) in order to make ends meet.

Indeed, by carrying the major share of household tasks and assigning them to daughters and other female kin, women help shape the reproduction of the working class along gender lines. This is accompanied by enhancement of their husbands' class positions since less time spent in the home gives husbands more opportunities to look for better jobs and bargain and organize their labour. As we shall see, the nature of marital allocations of resources and exchange patterns between spouses have a direct influence on decision-making in the sexual arena.

NOTES

1. Control over household income is gauged from information gathered on respondents' knowledge and/or handling of (*a*) family income ('What is your monthly family income?'). A majority of women gave approximate estimates while some women could not give any. (*b*) Husband's income ('How much money does your husband earn at the end of the month/week/day?'/'What does he do with the money?'). Women either had full, partial or no knowledge of the incomes of husbands and cited different patterns of husbands' dealing with their incomes. (*c*) Own income ('What do you do with the money?' for women doing paid work only) Respondents described how their monthly incomes were spent.
2. Nature of family decision-making is evaluated from response to the question: 'If you and your husband are purchasing something for the house, or buying clothes or food, how do you go about it? Who makes the final decision?'
3. Husband's participation in housework is gauged from the question, 'Does your husband help with your housework?' 'How often?' (Responses given were: Frequently; Sometimes; When I ask him; Never), 'In What manner?'
4. Information about husband's drinking is elicited from response to the question,'Does your husband drink alcohol?' (if yes) 'How frequently?'
5. Information on wife beating is elicited from women's response to the question, 'Does he [meaning husband] hit you when he gets angry?'
6. Outlook and feelings about life are coded from the responses to the question,'Taking all things together, how do you feel about your family life?' (Probe for specific experiences, descriptions of feelings of obligations and duties, frustrations, optimism/pessimism, feelings about husband, children, money.) Responses given to an open-ended question such as this were, of course, varied. In the coding scheme, I underscored the most recurrent themes and the feelings and issues about which respondents were most emphatic.
7. Information regarding relaxation, outing and so on were elicited from the following question, (*a*) 'How many days a week do you work [implying paid work]?' (*b*) 'Do you get any holidays [implying days off from paid work]?') (*c*) 'On a typical day do you get any time to relax?'/ 'What do you do then?' (*d*) 'Do you get to chat with friends?' (*e*) 'Do you get to watch TV?' (if yes) 'How often?' (*f*) 'Do you get to see cinemas in movie halls?' (*g*) 'Do you get to listen to the radio?' (*h*) 'Do you ever go for outings with your husband/children/relatives/friends, say to the zoo, museum, Victoria Memorial, places outside of Calcutta and so on?' Observation of respondents' daily schedules also contributed to the understanding of their situations.

4

Articulation of Love and Sexual Interactions

Most demographic studies on sexual behaviour focus on quantifiable aspects of 'coital frequency' in order to facilitate contraceptive intervention (Nag 1996). The preoccupation is with issues like risk of conception, fecundity and ovulation, all considered useful for understanding contraceptive-use dynamics in terms of management of family planning programmes (Blanc and Rutenberg 1991:162) and revealing some aggregate data on sexual behaviour patterns. Women, however, are considered primarily as means of reproduction instead of active reproductive and sexual human beings. Accordingly, consideration of coital frequency completely overlooks issues of autonomy and conflicting gender interests which affect the sexual act.

Indeed, women's articulations of sexuality and sexual relations are a form of expressing control over their bodies and over their fertility. Since very little is known about the material dynamics of poor working class women's sexual agency in India (Mencher 1989: 119), I focus here upon the nature of these articulations in the working class context of the women's lives, establishing the links between wives' limited control over intra-household resource allocation and their negotiation of intimate spheres of conjugal dynamics like love and sexual relations. The confines of wives' agency in sexual interactions reveal the ramifications of societal gender construction within the working class.

EXPRESSION AND DYNAMICS OF INTIMACY: SOME GENERAL IMPRESSIONS

For women in the sample, sexual interaction was typically associated with initiation of the marital relationship. Due to the taboo generally attached to premarital sex in India, I was forbidden by social workers to ask women directly about it. Instead of deleting the question altogether, however, I decided to ask it in an indirect manner: 'Prior to marriage did the female elders in your family/friends ever tell you or did you know from any experience about how you should get intimate with your husband, how you get children and so on?' When asked about any knowledge or experience in premarital sexual relations the women essentially said they 'came to know of these things only after marriage'. Even among those (18%) who reported having a 'love' marriage (as against a marriage 'arranged' by seniors in the family), the romance was described in terms of 'going to the cinema with other friends', 'talking to each other on the road', or just 'exchanging glances which led to love . . . but never the things which one has to do after marriage'. For instance, Maina described her experience as follows:

> 'I would go to fetch water and he would be standing there every day, waiting for me. Most of the time, I would walk away, averting my eyes but one day, I looked up and smiled at him. The following day, he came up and asked me where I was working. He was quite good-looking then [laughs] and I liked talking with him. So I told him where I was working. Then he said, "Will you come to watch *Muquaddar ka Sikandar* tomorrow?" I was scared but agreed and the next day, though still scared, I went. He was waiting for me. I began walking on one side of the street while he walked on the other. We walked in this manner until we reached the bus. Then we talked. It was always like this—we were very careful not to be seen in our locality with one another!'

Only one woman talked about some 'hand holding and kissing' in her premarital years. Part of the reticence regarding premarital sex can certainly be ascribed to the taboo attached to it in Indian society and, therefore, the innocent answer to my question must be taken with a pinch of salt. Nevertheless, the general ignorance and confusion about sex before marriage among women in the sample was fairly evident. Salma's account illustrates the point:

> 'Just after I got married, I did not know what was happening. I did not understand why my husband was behaving with me in that manner. After the first night, every time I saw his feet crossing the doorsteps through my veil, I started shivering and getting feverish. I was really scared of him. Then, when I came to my natal home, I told my mother and aunts, "I don't want to go back to him again!" They laughed at me and said, "You fool, you are married now, that's what happens when you are married, that's what all husbands do, that's normal. You have to be with him." They reasoned

with me and slowly I realized the whole thing. After that, I got used to my husband.'

Typically, therefore, sex is accepted as part of the marital contract, something that women have to reciprocate in their marital roles as wives. Most women in the study learnt to internalize the dynamics of this reciprocity soon enough after marriage. Acceptance of sex as a 'marital duty' is not surprising given that much of a woman's life-events are charted out by adults in their families of origin with the notion that ultimately, her marital role and duties will gain preeminence in her life. The realization that sex is an integral part of the same marital institution would, understandably, infuse acceptance and reciprocation of sex as a 'wifely duty' within marriage after the initial trauma and shock. And when sex is accepted as a marital duty more than anything else, it is not surprising that when asked, 'Do you love your husband?', 78 percent of the women across all ages replied that they did, because it is a wife's 'duty'.

How are these 'wifely duties' manifested in women's own notions of conjugal love and sex? To what extent are the women able to negotiate in their sexual interactions, given the wifely obligations they feel? Do women's expression of sexual agency vary on the basis of their monetary contributions to the household? Before addressing these questions, a description of the physical environment where sex takes place and some consequent factors influencing wives' feelings and responses pertaining to sexual encounters (with reference to the sample) are in order.

Descriptions of the women's rooming arrangements and living conditions (see Chapter 1), make it quite evident that in the cramped rooms and crowded surroundings of Calcutta's slums, sex can hardly be very private or intimate. In fact, only eight women and their husbands in the study sample had a room to themselves. The rest (92%) shared rooms with children and female kin. In some instances (48%), husbands slept outside in the courtyard, or alone in different sleeping areas either because they did not want to be 'bothered by sleeping next to the children after a hard day's work' or because lack of space required men to sleep outside. In other instances (20%), the wives and husbands slept with their children in between, either to protect the children from falling or because 'it does not look good if wives and husbands sleep next to each other in front of the children'. The lack of privacy being a given, it is not surprising that husbands communicate their initial desire for intercourse through nonverbal cues and gestures. Purni and Lolita's descriptions typify the sexual overtures encountered by the majority of women sleeping separately from their husbands.

> Purni: At night, he [my husband] comes into the room, say, with the pretext of drinking water and then coughs a little bit. And I know that he wants to have sex (*showa bosha kortay chay*—literally, sleeping, sitting work). So I have to get up, and go to the floor, *finish the work* [my emphasis] and go back to bed.
>
> Lolita: On some days, he will bring special food for dinner and I know that he wants it. So on those nights, I will sleep on his side of the bed or on the floor with him for the first half of the night, *do the work* [my emphasis] and then go back to my place again.

While a majority (73%) of the women appear to feel that sex is an assigned 'work' (*showa boshar kaj/sonay baythnay ka kam*) that has to be done,[1] the 'public' nature of the act also generates a considerable amount of tension. Of the hundred women in the sample, only nineteen (including the eight who have a room to themselves) were either alone in the room or had very small children who did not make them feel self-conscious. Additionally, eight wives had not been sexually active over the past six months. The remainder (73%) admitted that they were extremely tense during sex, fearing that their growing children or kin would wake up and see. From all accounts, this tension was not as pervasive among the husbands, as half of these women stated that their husbands did not care 'at all' about other people watching. Rehana, who shared the same room with her husband, eighty-year-old mother and four children aged twelve to eighteen, talked about her predicament:

> 'My mother is very old and she cannot sleep at night. So she can see everything that we are doing if she looks our way. I tell my husband, "Do your work fast and get off. Mother can see." He says, "If she has no problem watching, I have no problem doing it. You are my wife, I can do anything with you!" When I get angry at this and try to protest, he slaps me.'

Overall, then, women's agency in the negotiation of intimacy seems to be severely constrained by the limits of their physical environment and compounded by the gender dynamics of spousal roles.

Several micro-level studies on India provide useful insights on the cultural determinants of sexuality and sexual norms. Wadley (1977) shows how the dominant Hindu cultural ideology finds the female fertile and benevolent when men get control of her sexuality, and potentially malevolent and destructive when in control of her own sexuality. Hindu scriptures give guidance on protecting female children's virginity until marriage (Das 1985). Accordingly, women are socialized into maintaining chastity and purity of their bodies (Carroll 1983; Das 1985). Men, on the other hand, are socialized into authoritarian, demanding and initiating roles (Poffenberger and Poffenberger 1973). Sexual double standards are, thus, a basis of the gender dynamics of spousal roles. Emphasis on motherhood as noble and God-given implicitly directs women to perform sexual activity which, of course, should lead to reproduction and perpetuation of the patriarchal family lineage (Mandelbaum 1974; Wadley 1977; Mukhopadhyay and Savithri 1998).

Indeed, psychoanalytic studies suggest that the accent on motherhood undermines notions of conjugality central to male and female relationships (Nandy 1980: 41). There is a general reticence to talk about sex in the Indian ethos. While an analysis of cultural determinants elucidates some aspects of women's position in Indian society, it fails to convey a sense of women's agency in the sexual process. It overlooks the conflicts and contradictions which may arise in a sexual encounter.

In the early nineties, Kakar's incisive psychoanalytical study on Indian sexuality revealed some of the gender conflicts inherent in sexual relations among couples. Of particular interest to this research are his case studies of the 'hopes, wishes, fantasies and conflicts' (Kakar 1990:65) of two urban slum-dwelling women. Here, Kakar explicitly reveals the mundane realities of sex in a cramped room as well as the dynamics of emotion, power and kin relations which influence the clashing sexual interests of the wife and the husband. Kakar's explanation of the issues, precludes discussion of material bases for the behaviour and dwells upon Freudian and Jungian analysis of Indian culture. Roldan's study (1988 : 240) on the material and social basis of conjugal interactions within working class households, on the other hand, shows that even when women contribute more than 40 percent of household expenses, their husbands, in most cases, decide if and when to have sexual intercourse. In the Indian context, however, hardly any studies documenting women's autonomy in sexual relations and/or the material factors influencing these relations seem to exist (Mencher 1989: 119). Contexts within which sexual behaviour occurs have also been largely ignored by those involved in family planning (Nag 1996).

Consequently, in order to understand the essence of the wives' sexual negotiations, I asked them several questions: 'How is love expressed between you and your husband?' ('Probe: Is it more mental, physical or both?') 'Do/did you ever initiate sex with your husband?' (If yes) 'How?' (If no) 'Why not?' 'When intercourse is over, how do you feel?' ('Probe: Do you feel satisfied?') 'Do you get to know how your husband feels?' ('Probe: Does he feel satisfied?') Further, in order to gauge the conjugal dynamics pertaining to the husbands' application of force or threat of force and the nature of the women's response to the demands made by the husbands the women were asked, 'What happens when your husband wants to have sex and you don't feel like it?' Let us find out what their replies unfold in the context of their position in the phase of family cycle and across household income allocation groups (A, B, C [pooling continuum] and D and E [housekeeping allowance sets]).

LOVE AND SEXUAL INITIATION

HOUSEHOLDS IN THE EARLY PHASE OF FAMILY CYCLE[2]

For a majority of wives across all household income allocation groups (A, B, C, D, and E) in this phase, exchanges in love are separate from that in sex. In the eyes of wives, spousal love is mainly expressed through domestic exchanges in day-to-day cohabitation: 'Love for husband comes from living with him and being married to him, like it can be when you are living with anyone for some time.' Fragments of women's responses to the question 'How is love expressed between the two of you [husband and wife]?' illustrate the point:

'I look after him, arrange for his food. If I don't have money I borrow food for him from somewhere. He brings in money when he can. That is how love is expressed between the two of us.'

'I give him food, massage his legs with oil, wash clothes. He does not show any physical affection. So I don't show any affection either. I just do what I have to. I guess that is love.'

Indication of love waning is also seen in the context of material exchange, as Joya's description of marital love shows:

'When he loves me he brings things like a saree and this and that. When he hates me he says, "I won't bring anything."'

On the wife's part, therefore, loving may be significantly dissociated from sexual intercourse. Love is not necessarily perceived or expressed as a component of sexual interaction.

Accordingly, a majority of the wives within all income allocation groups do not initiate intercourse. Wives maintained that they 'feel very tired after the day's work and don't feel like' having intercourse or 'feel shy since women are not supposed to ask for it'. Thus, sexual intercourse is primarily considered a 'physical function' bereft of any romantic notions commonly found in Indian media portrayals of sex.

HOUSEHOLDS IN THE ADULT PHASE OF FAMILY CYCLE

With regard to expressions of love, women in the adult cycle varied across the pooling continuum and housekeeping allowance set. The only woman in the pooling continuum in Group A, maintained that the basis of her 'love' for her husband was 'mental' emerging from living with him and building up a household for so many years. A similar attitude about 'loving', articulated through conjugal reciprocities in daily running of the household, is expressed by a majority (80%) of older wives not currently engaged in paid work (Group E).

'Husbands [on the other hand] only love what all men love in women and it is only apparent at night.' Older wives in Group B (75%) and Group C (50%) in the pooling continuum and wives in Group D (50%) in the housekeeping allowance set, thus, have a more openly cynical attitude about love. Predominantly, for them, exchange of conjugal love, is not manifested through reciprocities in day-to-day living. Rather, these wives feel that while they do their duties towards their husbands — working, giving them food and washing their clothes — love of husbands towards their wives is confined to the physical domain. Seemingly, with age and experience, wives in these subgroups go beyond dissociating sex from love as their younger counterparts did. In fact, they perceive sex more overtly as a commodity of exchange demanded by their husbands as a marital prerogative. Given this perception, it is not surprising that, like their younger counterparts, the majority of wives across all income-allocation groups do not initiate intercourse.

SATISFACTION WITH SEXUAL INTERCOURSE

Some Western feminist literature has made significant contributions towards understanding gender conflicts inherent in sexual and contraceptive behaviour. Sexual interactions between spouses are identified as potential areas of conflict as the path-breaking studies of England and Farkas (1986) and Pollack (1985) have shown. Pollack has also shown that for men, sexual gratification is all-important; they tend to dissociate themselves from the consequences of sexual intercourse. These attitudes have far-reaching consequences in terms of contraceptive-use dynamics.

In Table 4.1, which shows the patterns of sexual satisfaction expressed by wives in the pooling continuum and housekeeping allowance sets, only a modal group (40%) among wives in Group A say they feel good after sex.[3] Another 40 percent feel 'nothing' or just plain 'tired after a long day's work'. Recall that wives in this group have to do with an average of five and a half hours of sleep every night. The latter response, therefore, is not surprising.

Feelings of satisfaction after intercourse were not voiced by a majority of wives in any of the other pooling or housekeeping allowance sets. In fact, a modal group (38.9%) of the wives in Group B felt repulsed and angry after intercourse. Sabita, a wife in Group B, elaborates:

> 'When he touches me, I feel repulsed and angry. I shut my eyes and think of all things holy. I think of gods and goddesses. I hate it when that white thing comes out and makes me wet—it's such a horrible feeling!'

Perhaps, the fact that wives like Sabita gain very little in terms of economic contributions from their husbands, they are more open about expressing anger at their husbands' demands. But then the majority of the wives who contribute less than 40 percent to the pool (Group C) and those in the housekeeping allowance sets (Groups D and E) feel much the same way as Lolita's comments reveal:

> 'Satisfaction? You must be joking. What is there to feel satisfied about? I feel exhausted and empty. You tell me, after cooking, fetching water, cleaning and washing clothes, can anyone enjoy this torture.'

Table 4.1 Wife's Satisfaction with Sexual Intercourse* by Income Allocation Groups

	Satisfied	Exhausted/ No Feeling	Repulse/ Angry	Total (n)
Group A Wife contributes > 40%, husband stable provider	40 (2)	40 (2)	20 (1)	100.0 (5)
Group B Wife contributes > 40% husband unstable provider	22.2 (4)	38.9 (7)	38.9 (7)	100.0 (18)
Group C Wife contributes < 40% husband stable provider	36 (9)	52 (13)	12 (3)	100.0 (25)
Group D Wife's money not used for household expenses, husband gives allowance	-	60 (3)	40 (2)	100.0 (5)
Group E Wife does not earn, husband gives allowance	30.3 (10)	45.5 (15)	24.2 (8)	100.0 (33)

*Excludes those who said don't know and those abstaining from intercourse.

How, in the eyes of the women, do the husbands feel about sex? Overwhelmingly, a majority of women within both pooling and housekeeping allowance groups echoed their normative outlooks about men's sexuality. Consequently, a wife's typical response was, 'He likes it, he is a man.' The women's feelings about sex were varied, however. Barring the few wives in the young group who say that they find sex satisfying, what happens during sexual intercourse to warrant the subdued expressions of sexuality on the part of wives—both in terms of initiation and satisfaction? Are women's outlooks about husbands' enjoyment of sex 'being a man' in any way conditioned by the sexual agency expressed by a majority of husbands during intercourse?

CONJUGAL DYNAMICS DURING SEXUAL INTERCOURSE

In order to gauge some of these issues pertaining to the dynamics of differential conjugal autonomy during intercourse, wives were asked to describe what happened when their husbands wanted to have sexual intercourse, but the wives did not. From the range of responses of wives to this query, three types of sexual scenarios seemed to emerge:

(*a*) Husbands do not apply any force once the wives tell them that they do not feel like having intercourse ('I tell him, and he listens,' is a typical response of wives).
(*b*) Husbands apply force or threat of force and/or desertion to persuade wives. In these circumstances actions of husbands range from lifting the wife from the bed and putting her down on the floor while she is half asleep and muttering, 'no', to just threatening to either leave or apply force because 'wives are *supposed* [my emphasis] to do these things'. Incidentally, the concept of marital rape being non-existent, forced sex within a marriage cannot be and is not viewed as such.
(*c*) Husbands do not actively apply force or verbal threats. Rather, the wives are apprehensive and cautious not to displease their husbands. In these cases, husbands do not even get to know what wives want ('I don't tell him that I don't feel like it. I don't want to make him unhappy. He works so hard all day.')

Do these situations vary on the basis of wives' income contribution in the household? As in Table 4.1, in Table 4.2, which depicts the varied conjugal dynamics at work during intercourse across income-allocation groups, the patterns across young and adult phases of family cycle can be considered similar unless mentioned otherwise. Within the pooling continuum, a majority (66.7%) of husbands in Group A, do not force their wives to have intercourse. This is also the group where a modal response included enjoyment of sex by wives. Recall, that these households are also relatively egalitarian and open with regard to making family decisions and to control over income. Unfortunately, the only wife in the adult cycle who is in Group A, had not been sexually active for the previous four months. She and her husband considered themselves old enough to 'to stop those things [sexual intercourse]'. Thus, she does not feature in the foregoing discussion.

Table 4.2 Nature of Conjugal Dynamics During Sexual Intercourse by Income-Allocation Groups

	Husband does not need to force wife since she does not express displeasure even when she feels it	Husband uses force or threat of force, and/or desertion	Husband does not use force, listens to wife	No Sex	Total (n)
Group A Wife contributes > 40%, husband stable provider	-	16.7 (1)	66.7 (4)	16.7 (1)	100.0 (6)
Group B Wife contributes > 40% husband unstable provider	4.5 (1)	54.5 (12)	31.8 (7)	9.1 (2)	100.0 (22)
Group C Wife contributes < 40% husband stable provider	26.9 (7)	42.3 (11)	26.9 (7)	3.8 (1)	100.0 (26)
Group D+E Housekeeping allowance set	27.9 (12)	41.9 (18)	20.9 (9)	9.3 (4)	100.0 (43)

The pattern of conjugal dynamics during intercourse alters in the pooling Group B. Interestingly, two of the wives in the young phase in this group were abstaining from sexual intercourse for a month preceding the interviews, because they did not think they 'need to do these things anymore, with someone who is a husband for namesake and does not do his duties to provide for the household.' Additionally, in seven cases (31.8%), husbands do not apply force or threat of force. However, all wives in this group, are not able to assert their sexual agency during intercourse. In fact, in twelve cases (a little over half, i.e., 54.5%), husbands still exert force or threat of force. Perhaps, loss of control of the economic domain to their wives, induces husbands in this group to regain some autonomy by exercising control over their wives' sexuality.

Bijoya's comment about her experience with her husband during intercourse illustrates the point:

> 'I don't like all this sex. So he always has to force me when he wants me to sleep with him. Just like that, he could never convince me. He loves to do it [have sex]. He tells me that so many people are doing it. I say, 'So what, I have to work harder than others, I feel tired.' He says, 'Working doesn't matter, you are lying here next to me, you are a wife, you are here for this. You have to do it also.'

The exercise of force in sexual negotiation evident in Bijoya's account leads to intense conflict during intercourse in some cases. Chhipli, a mother of three boys, working as a domestic servant and living with her mother-in-law and unemployed husband had this to say about her situation:

> 'Initially, I went along with it [husband's wish to have sex] because this is natural between husbands and wives. But I am so tired after the day's work, I cannot really put up with it. So I started saying no. He abuses me, has slapped me quite a few times for saying no but now I just sit tight in the corner of the room.'

Thus, similar to the dynamics of exchange of household labour (see Chapter 3), paid work and virtual breadwinner status of wives do not necessarily foster egalitarian sexual exchange. Rather, wives try to forge minimum means of autonomy to counter their husbands' demands for sex.

The pattern of conjugal dynamics seems to alter to some extent for wives in the pooling continuum Group C and the housekeeping allowance set, whose husbands are also the main economic providers (Groups D and E).[4] The exercise of force or threat of force and desertion is still the modal description in all three of these subgroups as conveyed by the comment of a Sumitra in Group D: 'He says "if I don't, I can always pay five bucks to the woman on the pavement and do the work with her!"' But more than a quarter of the wives in Groups C, D and E also do not express their unwillingness to have intercourse even if they do not feel like it, in fear that they will displease their husbands. For them, the annoyance of husbands is potentially costly, as the following comments suggest 'I don't say anything. He works very hard, I can't make him unhappy.' 'I keep quiet and bear it. Who will feed my children if I displease him?' Note that women in these three groups earn considerably less than their husbands, if they do so at all, and are, therefore, more dependent upon husbands' incomes than the wives in the other subgroups (Groups A and B). Consequently, the emerging pattern in wives' apprehensions about displeasing the husband may be seen as a strategy devised to protect their households' economic interests. Indeed, one can find an almost bell-shaped pattern emerging in the conjugal negotiations pertaining to refusal of sexual intercourse by young wives in the pooling continuum and housekeeping allowance sets (see Figure 4.1).

Fig.4.1 Sexual Coercion as the Balance of Economic Contribution Shifts

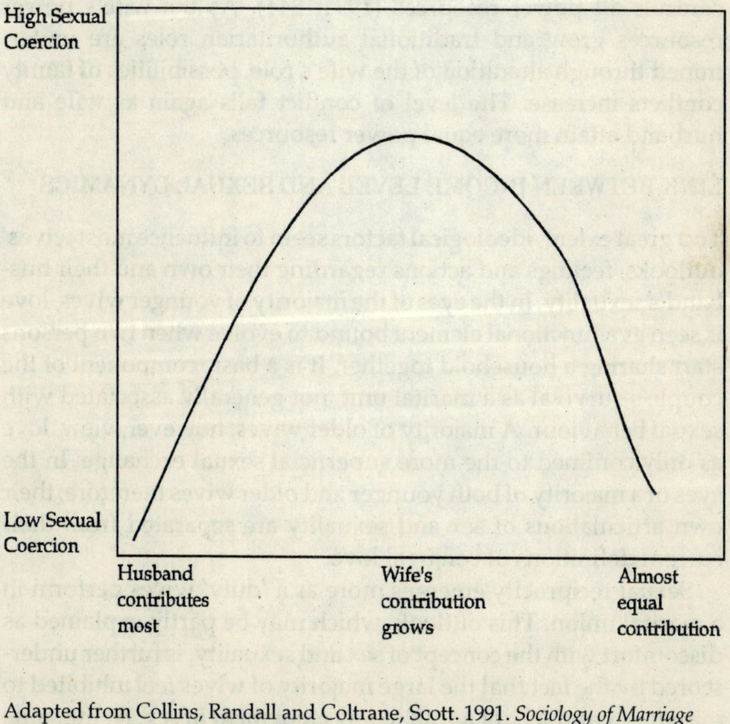

Adapted from Collins, Randall and Coltrane, Scott. 1991. *Sociology of Marriage and the Family: Gender, Love and Property*. Chicago : Nelson-Hall Publishers, 645

To the extent that there is an emerging pattern to suppress the feelings of wives in Groups C, D and E, a majority of their husbands, who are also the main economic providers, do not need to exercise coercion during sexual encounters. Coercion in sexual encounters becomes the dominant pattern when husbands lose their economic provider status and their wives' incomes are seen as becoming more and more crucial to the survival of the household (Group B). Thus, as the women gradually break away from normative roles and infiltrate into traditionally male domains, renegotiation of sexual relations becomes increasingly conflict-ridden. Predominance of coercion falls again and things stabilize around a more egalitarian situation when wives contribute substantially to the household along with husbands (Group A) and the income gaps between husbands and wives decrease. Wives are now able slowly to re-negotiate sexual control with their husbands. This pattern coincides with Collins and Coltrane's contention that level of conjugal conflict is low when husband controls all power resources (1991: 244). As the wife's power resources grow and traditional authoritarian roles are undermined through alteration of the wife's role, possibilities of family conflicts increase. The level of conflict falls again as wife and husband attain more equal power resources.

LINK BETWEEN INCOME LEVEL AND SEXUAL DYNAMICS

To a great extent, ideological factors seem to influence most wives' outlooks, feelings and actions regarding their own and their husband's sexuality. In the eyes of the majority of younger wives, love is seen as a functional element bound to evolve when two persons start sharing a household together. It is a basic component of the couple's survival as a marital unit, not generally associated with sexual behaviour. A majority of older wives, however, view love as only confined to the more superficial sexual exchange. In the eyes of a majority of both younger and older wives therefore, their own articulations of sex and sexuality are separated from their current definitions of conjugal love.

Sexual reciprocity emerges more as a 'duty' wives perform in a marital union. This outlook, which may be partly explained as discomfort with the concept of sex and sexuality, is further underscored by the fact that the large majority of wives feel inhibited to initiate sex and do not admit to any enjoyment of sex. At the same time, a majority of the women are convinced that their husbands being male enjoy sex. Evidently, a 'gendered' construction of sexuality appears to be expressed by women. In their eyes, men are legitimate aggressors and wives are more passive. In this sense the women's world views reflect the traditional Indian pattern of sexuality among males and females (Chaudhury 1990). These articulations and attitudes of women in the study are partly understandable in the context of the historical milestones that influenced the women's life-chances (see Chapter 1). Thus, given the overwhelming dominance of 'domesticated' spheres in the women's lives since the period of their older childhood socialization, and the fact that they have almost no knowledge or experience of premarital sex, it is not surprising that women tend to condone passive sexuality as more legitimate for their gender.

As discussed in the Introduction, the Gender and Development (GAD) perspective is an appropriate framework within which to analyse gender asymmetries by linking relations of productive and reproductive labour and emphasizing the impact of this double burden on women's lives. Keeping the GAD framework in mind, then, in addition to ideology, what other factors may be linked to the women's apparent reluctance to engage in sex and their physical and mental fatigue after sex? The women have ten- to sixteen- hour workdays on the average (see Chapter 3). Given this rigorous schedule, it is understandable that the majority of women do not want to encounter intercourse or cannot enjoy the experience in the cramped rooms with little privacy: the whole process does not seem to afford any physical or mental relaxation. Thus, contrary to popular stereotypes about sex as recreation for the poor in India, women's articulations in and about sexual behaviour show that sexual interactions are hardly recreational, at least for a poor working class woman. For instance, after a long hard day of work, one woman felt that sexual intercourse is an additional task that she had to deal with on a creaky bed with children sleeping by her side. For another woman, it was on the damp floor, smelling the alcohol on her husband's breath while the mother-in-law sighed on the bed above. Thus, sexual passivity cannot be ascribed only to ideology. Rather, ideology is created, recreated and perpetuated as the material realities of women's lives take shape.

Also, at a relative level, descriptions of the women's sexual interactions show that to some extent the nature of negotiation is linked to a wife's economic dependence on her husband. Wives who make substantial contributions to household expenses (Group A, young cycle; see Chapter 3) seem to be the only group in a position of relative power to have open negotiations with husbands about sexual interactions and, consequently are more likely to enjoy sex as well. In this instance, paid work, specifically women's higher contribution in the pool gives some women a few areas of control and power, however asymmetrical the conjugal exchanges might seem to an outsider. But for wives emerging as main earners of their households with their husbands becoming irregular providers (Group B), the latter's coercion in the sexual domain is still very much a reality. These wives' displeasure in their husbands' actions is only expressed through their repulsion and anger at sexual intercourse.

Two patterns of conjugal dynamics emerge among both young and adult wives relatively more dependent upon their husbands for their family's and children's material well-being (Groups C, D and E). One dominant trait, is that husbands have the power to exercise force or threat of force/desertion to induce wives to have sexual intercourse against their wishes. The other emerging pattern, absent in Groups A and B, is that some wives contributing less than 40 percent of household expenses, may be so anxious not to displease their husbands, that they may not even voice their reluctance to have intercourse. In these instances, the sexual interaction takes place without any apparent coercion applied by husbands. However, the wife's wish remains unheard. As noted before, these wives are more economically dependent upon their husbands for their familial well-being. The latter is the primary preoccupation of the majority (68%) of the wives in this sample. Under such circumstances, it is perhaps natural that where husbands have to be depended upon for economic support, women have to take into consideration the husband's wishes during sexual negotiations.

To say, therefore, that women in the sample are only passive sexual agents would undermine much of the agency they exercise to protect their gender interests. Women in the sample actually emerge as active strategists, attempting within their limited means to slowly re-negotiate with their husbands and forge a space of sexual control, simultaneously keeping in mind the collective well-being of their families. This revelation points to the necessity to look beyond cultural explanations of Indian women's sexual passivity so abundant in mainstream demographic studies

(Nag 1972; Chaudhury 1990; George 1993) and to focus on links between women's sexual articulations and intra-household allocation and control of resources within particular social class contexts.

What do the women's sexual interactions portend in terms of societal formation of gender beyond the household level? The explorations show that the construction of sexuality and sexual articulations both at the ideological and material levels, and at the level of dialectics between the ideological and material, help to perpetuate women's subordination. Women's limited sexual prerogatives are illustrated by their perception of sexual interactions as wifely duty, by the minimal control they have over their bodies during intercourse and, ultimately, by the overwhelming exhaustion and emptiness they feel after sexual intercourse. These elements of subordination are further underscored by women's participation in less secure and stable occupations, lower incomes, lesser monetary contribution and control over their own incomes in the household, in relation to their husbands.

What is more, intergenerational reproduction of societal processes unfolding through differential treatment of gender serve to perpetuate women's oppression as a gender, in general, and subordination of their sexuality and spheres of their sexual experiences, in particular.

What is perceived to be at odds with women's interests in feminist theory is not necessarily so for poor working class women. Since these women's access to and control of resources is limited by the historical processes of class and gender formation, women may not find it in their interest to abolish their 'wifely duties' or the domestic and sexual exchanges, processes, which the theoretical framework in this study projects as reflecting inequality. Women might want to change the dimensions of the reciprocities, say, for instance, in sexual exchange, according to their current definitions of a 'proper' marital relationship, but never do away with the dynamics altogether. This is certainly true for women in the sample as Rani's introspection about her sexual life and marriage conveys:

> 'During sex, he treats me like a prostitute. He wants everything I have. If I say that to him, he beats me. I don't know if all men are like that. All I want, is a little respect. See, we have been together this long. We have been through so much. We have a son. So

> obviously, I care for him and I can't really leave him! I cannot live alone and bring up my son! What will I do not being married? If only he could show me some respect.'

Thus, much of the women's means of sustenance at a social and economic level and meaning of existence as human beings rests on their current household situations. And as Beneria and Roldan (1987:163) point out:

> This lack of congruence between working-class women's concrete gender and class reality and the conceptualization of gender interests formulated at a more abstract level of analysis posits a fundamental challenge to feminist theory and decision-making.

In spite of its assumed claim to universality, feminist theory can be quite irrelevant when applied directly in the context of a working class woman. Where the theory is relevant is in the perception — under the GAD rubric — of women as active, rather than passive, participants in the development process. This insight can have a potentially far-reaching impact upon the quality and effectiveness of development initiatives undertaken. More specifically, an understanding of the relationship between intra-household income allocation and sexual dynamics and decision-making within the household, can be effectively utilized in fashioning more effective population control programmes.

NOTES

1. This conclusion is reached from context analysis of women's responses to questions about expression of love and satisfaction with sex.
2. Includes women in nuclear and extended households in the early phase with female children below 18 years and male children below 21 years.
3. Includes only those wives in the young phase of family cycle since the only wife in the adult phase in this subgroup was abstaining from sexual intercourse at the time of the survey.
4. Due to the similarity in responses, the housekeeping allowance sets are collapsed in Table 4.2.

5
NEGOTIATING BIRTH CONTROL

Feminist theory repeatedly postulates the issue of men's control over women's fertility stating that 'the social relations which govern human reproductive behaviour serve to reflect, instil or reinforce the subordination of women' (Vock 1988: 83; Mukhopadhyay and Savithri 1998). In real life situations, the closely spaced births of women in developing countries is said to be an indicator of male control (Anker 1982). It is widely noted that although women's groups and family planning agencies stress the need for women to have control over their bodies and the reproductive process, theories of demography and empirical research on fertility differentials, with some exceptions, have largely ignored these issues (ibid.; Vock 1988).

Let us consider the links between wives' limited control over intra-household resource allocation and the renegotiation of gender relations inherent in their birth control trajectories. At first, however, I explore how wives' access to specific forms of birth control and consequent contraceptive choices are circumscribed by methods made available by the government (since typically, all women in the sample are only familiar with the free birth control methods and items promoted by the centralized family planning programme). Next, I turn to a description of wives' negotiations with their husbands on matters relating to birth control and its ramifications in terms of societal gender and class formation processes.

CHOOSING A CONTRACEPTIVE METHOD: HOW MANY OPTIONS?

Contraceptive-use dynamics outlined in concordance with coital frequency patterns (Blanc and Rutenberg 1991) preclude any consideration of women's control over the contraceptive decision-making process or the inconveniences of using prevalent contraceptives. Moreover, some studies on contraceptive behaviour in India simplistically perceive contraceptive usage only as an outcome of 'modernization' (Srinivasan et. al. 1984; Ramu 1988). Later studies have looked into the historical processes of household, class, gender formation that make the birth control decision-making process infinitely more complex (Dasgupta et al. 1995).

Initial investigation and pilot interviews indicated that: (*i*) poor women, like the respondents, are most likely to obtain methods and contraceptives freely distributed by the government. Specifically, sterilization (both male and female), pills, IUD (Intra-Uterine Devices) and condoms, the main methods promoted by the West Bengal Family Welfare Programme, are obtained from government institutions (hospital, urban health care centres) and approved voluntary organizations. This was true for women in the study. (*ii*) None of the respondents were familiar with or ever practised birth control with the aid of 'jelly', 'foam tablets' and 'cervical caps', some of the other methods promoted by the government.

One prominent aspect of the birth control trajectories of women in the sample is that 51 of them had obtained sterilization (tubectomy/laparoscopy) while a majority of the rest expressed their desire to do so in the near future.[1] As shown in Table 5.1, more than a quarter of the wives in the youngest age group (15–24 years) are sterilized, while 36.8 percent wish to be in the near future. Again, more than half (52.5%) of the wives in the 25 to 35 years age group and a majority (70%) of wives in the oldest age group (over 35 years), have undergone sterilization. Thus, even though the percentage of wives who were not thinking of sterilization or felt that they could not obtain sterilization due to religious prohibition[2] is quite substantial in each of the age-groups, the combined percentages of sterilized wives and those planning to obtain sterilization in the near future far exceeds the former. Seemingly, therefore, a tubectomy or laparoscopic sterilization are the most viable methods of contraception for the majority of women across all age groups.

What kind of difference does the number of living children make to this pattern? Table 5.1 shows that a majority (57.1%) of the women who did not have any children at the time of the interview were not thinking of sterilization.[3] However, a substantial percentage (42.9%) of them were already thinking about it. This pattern becomes more visible as women begin to have children.

Once again, the combined percentages of wives (with one to two, three to four and more than four children) having undergone sterilization and wishing to do so exceeds that of wives who did not think of sterilization as a viable contraceptive option.

Table 5.1 Female Sterilization Pattern by Age (%)

Age	Received Sterilization	Intend to Receive Sterilization	Not thought / Cannot*	Total (n)
15-24	26.3 (5)	36.8 (7)	36.9 (7)	100.0 (19)
25-35	52.5 (32)	16.4 (10)	31.2 (19)	100.0 (61)
36+	70.0 (14)	5.0 (1)	25 (5)	100.0 (20)
Number of Living Children (%)				
0**	-	42.9 (3)	57.1 (4)	100.0 (7)
1-2	33.3 (9)	29.6 (8)	37.0 (10)	100.0 (27)
3-4	66.7 (30)	13.3 (6)	20.0 (9)	100.0 (45)
5+	57.1 (12)	4.8 (1)	38.1 (8)	100.0 (21)

* Muslim women forbidden by religion to undergo sterilization.

** Includes Hindu women only. None of the Muslim women were childless. Thus, this group is not forbidden by religion to undergo sterilization.

It may be argued that as Hindu and Muslim women have a basic difference in their contraceptive selections in that some Muslim women expressed their inability to obtain sterilization due to religious decree (mostly conveyed to them by their husbands, mothers-in-law and in one case, the local religious head), clumping sterilization patterns of all women reflect a Hindu bias. Also, one cannot conclusively comment upon the preponderance of sterilization as the most viable option without comparing it with *other* birth control methods adopted by both Hindu and Muslim women. Do these factors make any difference to the foregoing tendency of a majority of women to opt for female sterilization?

Table 5.2 shows that even when compared across religion the majority of both Hindu and Muslim women tend to select female sterilization. The religious ban on sterilization seems to affect the decisions of a little less than one-third of the Muslim women in the sample. When broken down by number of children the pattern does not alter. Percentage of Muslim women who are sterilized or intend to do so still exceeds that of those rejecting sterilization out of fear of religious and consequent communal retaliation. Thus, even when broken down by religion, the dominant pattern of obtaining female sterilization evident in the sample remains unaltered. What about the status of sterilization in comparison to other birth control method selection patterns?

Table 5.2 Female Sterilization Pattern by Religion and Number of Living Children (%)

Age	Received Sterilization	Intend to Receive Sterilization	Not Allowed	Not thought	Total (n)
Hindu	51.5 (34)	22.7 (15)	-	25.8 (17)	100.0 (66)
		Number of Living Children (%)			
0	-	42.9 (3)	-	57.1 (4)	100.0 (7)
1-2	33.3 (8)	29.2 (7)	-	37.5 (9)	100.0 (24)
3-4	77.8 (21)	16.8 (4)	-	7.4 (2)	100.0 (27)
5+	62.5 (5)	12.5 (1)	-	25.0 (2)	100.0 (8)
Muslim	50 (17)	8.8 (3)	32.4 (11)	8.8 (3)	100.0 (34)
		Number of Living Children (%)			
0	-	-	-	-	-
1-2	33.3 (1)	33.3 (1)	-	33.3 (1)	100.0 (3)
3-4	50.0 (9)	11.1 (2)	33.3 (6)	5.6 (1)	100.0 (18)
5+	53.9 (7)	-	38.5 (5)	7.7 (1)	100.0 (13)

Note: In the 1-2 and 3+ children groups, the category includes women who tried other non-terminal methods, abandoned them later due to failure, health-hazards and perceived risks and ultimately opted for female sterilization.

Table 5.3 shows that among Hindus, a majority (57.1%) of women with no living children do not use any form of birth control. Many (37.5%) women with one to two children and a majority (77.8%) of those with three to four and more than four children (75%) however, tend to opt for female sterilization. Among Muslim women, a similar pattern is discernible among those with three to four or more than four children (50% and 61.5%

sterilized respectively). Also, Table 5.3 indicates, firstly, that the women are most likely not to opt for any contraception till they have at least one or two children. Even when women have one or two children, the percentage using non-terminal methods of birth control is relatively low. On the other hand, the percentage of unprotected couples (those not seeking any contraception) remains substantial across all groups. This does not bode well either for women's health or for population control.[4]

Table 5.3 Birth Control Method Choice Patterns by Religion and Number of Living Children (%)

	Hindu				Muslim			
	Number of Living Children				Number of Living Children			
Birth Control Method Choice	0	1-2	3-4	5+	0	1-2	3-4	5+
No birth control used	57.1 (4)	33.3 (8)	3.7 (1)	25.0 (2)	-	33.3 (8)	27.8 (5)	15.4 (2)
Some non-technical methods (includes pill, IUD, abortion, condom, withdrawal, rhythm, abstinence)	42.9 (3)	29.2 (7)	18.5 (5)	-	-	33.3 (1)	22.2 (4)	23.1 (3)
Female Sterilization	-	37.5 (9)	77.8 (21_	75.0 (6)	-	33.3 (1)	50.0 (9)	61.5 (8)
Total (n)	100.0 (7)	100.0 (24)	100.0 (27)	100.0 (8)	-	100.0 (3)	100.0 (18)	100.0 (13)

Note: In the 1-2 and 3+ children groups, the category includes women who tried other non-terminal methods, abandoned them later due to failure, health-hazards and perceived risks and ultimately opted for female sterilization.

Attempting to unravel the causes behind the high rate of 'non-use' is not within our purview. Speculatively, however, 'non-use' of contraception either reflects: (*i*) birth control behaviours of couples in a pronatal culture; or (*ii*) unmet needs of women (and their husbands) in the absence of adequate contraception; or (*iii*) dynamics of conjugal relations where one spouse is prevented by the other from obtaining or pursuing any form of contraception.[5] The majority option for female sterilization in the sample corresponds to national and state-level trends. What induces women (including those in the sample) to opt for female sterilization as the most viable method choice? After all, the government's free family planning clinic and hospital outlets visited by a majority of the women (and, sometimes, their husbands) offer a wider array of choices, including vasectomy (male sterilization), pills, condoms and IUD. Women's level of awareness on birth control choices would go some way in answering this question.

Women's sources of information on contraception range from 'other women in slum' to 'female kin', 'husband', 'hospital', 'health centre', 'village', 'radio and television'. Despite the varied sources, all women essentially referred to methods promoted and made available by the government. It must be emphasized that the centralized family planning programme in India has very aggressive and visible promotional tactics. Consequently, it is not surprising that such high percentages of women have 'heard of' female and male sterilization, abortion, IUD and condoms (Table 5.4). Comparison across groups shows however, that all women in the sample know of female sterilization as opposed to any other method of contraception. Seemingly, the majority of the women obtained or wanted to obtain the one method all the women had heard of: female sterilization. Interestingly, barring rhythm and withdrawal, two 'conventional' coitus-dependent contraceptive methods not overtly promoted by the family planning programme, the lowest percentage of women know about male contraception (both condom and sterilization). Additionally, even the 10.6-percent women who admitted knowledge of vasectomy procedures, were not able to give any satisfactory description of the process. Since all the birth control methods mentioned (except rhythm and withdrawal) are promoted by the same family planning programme, one may question whether the gender-differentiated information on birth control methods among the women reflects Basu's assertion that the government's programme promotes female procedures in general and female sterilization in particular to achieve its targets (1985: 425; Mukhopadhyay and Savithri 1998).

Despite being the most often heard of and commonly used method of birth control among the women, very few of them (18%) actually knew what the female sterilization 'operation' entails (Table 5.4). A typical response to the question regarding description of the procedure was, 'They made two braids with my hair, shaved me and made me unconscious'. In fact, of the 51 sterilized women in the sample, about a third underwent post-abortion sterilizations. Under these circumstances, the women were mostly in a situation where the question of finding out about the sterilization procedure did not arise. One of the respondents who went to have abortion without the knowledge of her husband said:

> 'When I went in for an abortion the doctors asked me how many children I had. I said, "Three." They said, "Then you should have an operation" [implying sterilization]. I agreed because at that point I could not afford to have another child. So if that meant having a sterilization I was ready to go for it. I did not have the time or energy to find out what this operation entailed. When you are in that state it is not possible to know and find out about these things.'

Table 5.4 Level of Awareness among Women on Birth Control Methods

Method	Heard of Method	Described Method	Correct Description among those who described method (%)
Female Sterilization	100 (100)	41 (41)	18 (17)
Male Sterilization	85 (85)	10.6 (9)	-
Medical Termination of Pregnancy (Abortion)	97 (97)	56.7 (55)	27.3 (15)
Pill	95 (95)	64.2 (61)	83.6 (51)
Intra-Uterine Devices (Loop, Copper T)	94 (94)	39.4 (37)	43.2 (51)
Condom	89 (89)	53.9 (48)	100 (48)
Rhythm	47 (47)	80.9 (38)	57.9 (22)
Withdrawal	45 (45)	100 (45)	100 (45)

This, once again, reflects the nature of control (or, more precisely, the lack thereof) the women actually have over the sterilization process. In an unspecified number of cases, women who went for abortion were even told that they would be charged to have an abortion but if it was followed by sterilization the entire procedure would be free of cost. In another instance, a woman recalled undergoing a tubectomy and then hearing a doctor admonishing the junior intern who performed the operation for 'tying the wrong tubes!' Consequently, she had to be operated upon once again. Although currently, the practice of providing monetary incentives for adopting the governments' family planning methods has been abolished at the time the study was conducted the National Family Planning Programme provided monetary incentives for those obtaining female (tubectomy and laparoscopic) and male (vasectomy) sterilization and IUD (Copper-T) insertion. The amount of money given for sterilization is higher, the highest being for laparoscopic sterilization (Government of West Bengal 1986: 31). Needless to say, the women in the sample received cash (most of the time) after obtaining sterilization. It is within this context of a veiled family planning programme bias that the birth control trajectories and nature of women's negotiations related to birth control must be understood.

WHY NOT VASECTOMY?

Thus, it is reasonably clear that whether it is a one-time attempt at contraception or a step taken after use of some non-terminal methods, female sterilization is perceived as the most viable birth control method choice by the majority of women in the sample. The question that obviously arises is that if the ultimate choice of a birth control method has to be terminal, why can it not be vasectomy, the simpler, less expensive and less cumbersome male sterilization procedure? As we saw, extant research has established some of the reasons for this overemphasis on female sterilization. Indeed, due to the family planning programme emphasis, the decline in vasectomy has been accompanied by a concomitant rise in tubectomy undermining the situation of women, particularly, poor illiterate women to a great extent (Basu 1985; Mukhopadhyay and Savithri 1998; Manna 1998). Very little, however, has been heard from women themselves regarding their views about vasectomy, in relation to their choice of tubectomy or laparoscopic sterilization. Nor has there been any attempt to show how women's particular household situations may be linked to these views.

In the present sample, none of the husbands had obtained or were going to obtain a vasectomy. The question that arises then is: Why do women settle for the relatively more cumbersome tubectomy/laparoscopy when it would be more prudent for their husbands to obtain vasectomies? Each respondent who at least knew of vasectomy, said 'no' when asked if her husband had obtained (or was going to obtain) a vasectomy. Then the question asked was: 'Why not?' (implying why did the husband not obtain a vasectomy). Typically the women's response to this question was accompanied by a rationale for their own sterilization. Again, there were some wives who had never heard of vasectomy along with those who thought that vasectomy did not exist anymore. Here are some typical responses:

> 'It is not good for the man to have that operation [vasectomy]. He is the one who earns and brings in the money. I am a woman. If something happens to me after the operation I can at least stay at home and do some work. In any case I cannot earn as much as he does. So if he is impaired by the operation my children will go without food.'

Some women even added:

> 'I don't/did not even know that vasectomy exists any more/at all and men can be operated upon. All I hear is that women can have the operation.'

For many Muslim women in the sample, the reason cited was:

> 'I tell him to get an operation since I am so weak. He says, "It's forbidden in the religion. I can't do it."'

Interestingly, despite the supposed religious ban, half of the Muslim women were sterilized and 8.8 percent were thinking of obtaining sterilization in the near future (see Table 5.2). None of the husbands, however, were sterilized. The ban therefore, seems to be applied more literally to sterilization decisions of Muslim husbands. All Muslim women who had obtained sterilization or were going to, admitted feeling guilty and upset at the thought that they may have committed a sin (*gunah*). However, there was nothing else the wives could do since they: (*i*) either did not know of any non-terminal methods; or (*ii*) were apprehensive of existing ones having heard about their potential health hazards; or (*iii*) the non-terminal methods they used had failed. Getting the husband to obtain a vasectomy was not a viable option.

Other reasons (among both Hindus and Muslims) included 'shyness' to tell the husband 'about these things' and desire to 'take charge' of birth control oneself without relying on the husband. As shown in Table 5.5, across all age groups the majority of women either feel that men should not obtain terminal birth control because they are the main economic providers and 'operation' might make them weak and incapacitated or the women are/were ignorant about the existence of vasectomy. Also, husbands of a substantial number (23%) of women in the 25 to 35 age range refused to obtain vasectomy when asked by wives. Among older women (more than 35 years), 70 percent of whom are sterilized (Table 5.1), the modal response (36.4%) was that their husbands' lives were not worth risking with vasectomy (while theirs were). A quarter (25.8%) of the women had also given up on the idea after their husbands refused to obtain sterilization.

Table 5.5 Reasons for Not Preferring Vasectomy by Ageand Number of Living Children

Age	Men are economic providers, better for women to obtain sterilization	Unaware vasectomy still exists/ exists at all	Husband's refusal (religious reasons cited for Muslims)	Want to take charge of birth control	Shy to tell husband	Total (n)
15-24	42.1 (8)	42.1 (8)	10.5 (2)	5.3 (1)	-	100.0
25-35	31.2 (19)	26.2 (16)	23 (14)	4.9 (3)	14.8 (9)	100.0
36+	50 (10)	25 (5)	15 (3)	10 (2)	-	100.0

Do monetary contributions of wives make any difference to this pattern? We look at the variations across income allocation groups by religion (Tables 5.6 and 5.7).

GROUP A

Among Hindu wives (who do not have any religious prohibitions regarding sterilization) the majority (60%) still seem to feel that men (being the main providers) should not opt for sterilization. Consequently, the responsibility for sterilization should dwell on women. Shafeen, the only Muslim woman in this group, was already sterilized. She had five living children and her husband never talked about vasectomy since the religious dictum against it was taken for granted. At the same time, she felt that she needed to control her fertility. So she discussed the possibilities of her own sterilization with her husband, taking the initiative to obtain sterilization despite knowing that 'it is a sin'.

Table 5.6 Reasons Given by Hindu Women for Not Preferring Vasectomy by Income Allocation Groups

Hindu	Group A Wife contributes > 40% Husband stable provider	Group B Wife contributes > 40% Husband unstable provider	Group C Wife contributes < 40% Husband stable provider	Group D Wife's money not used for household expenses Husband gives allowance	Group E Wife does not earn Husband gives allowances
Men economic providers, better for women to obtain sterilization	60.0 (3)	25.0 (5)	69.2 (9)	75.0 (3)	54.5 (12)
Unaware vasectomy still exists/ exists at all	40.0 (2)	35.0 (7)	23.1 (3)	-	31.8 (7)
Husband's refusal (religious reasons cited for Muslims)	-	5.0 (1)	-	-	4.5 (1)
Want to take charge of birth control	-	15.0 (3)	-	-	-
Shy to tell husband about birth control	-	20.0 (4)	7.8 (1)	25.0 (1)	9.1 (2)
Total* (n)	100.0 (5)	100.0 (0)	100.0 (13)	100.0 (4)	100.0 (22)

*Excludes 3 households where neither spouse was engaged in paid work at the time of the survey.

GROUP B

The major pattern in this subgroup is similar for both Hindu and Muslim women. Since husbands are not regular economic providers, the women do not seem to think that husbands' income-earning role should be a deterrent to vasectomy. Rather, most of the wives were ignorant of the existence of vasectomy. For a quarter of the Hindu wives, however, perception of the husband as the main income provider still dictated their gender differentiated birth control choices.

Table 5.7 Reasons Given by Muslim Women for Not Preferring Vasectomy by Income Allocation Groups

Muslim	Group A Wife contributes > 40% Husband stable provider	Group B Wife contributes > 40% Husband unstable provider	Group C Wife contributes < 40% Husband stable provider	Group D Wife's money not used for household expenses Husband gives allowance	Group E Wife does not earn Husband gives allowan-ces
Men economic providers, better for women to obtain sterilization	-	-	15.4 (2)	-	12.5 (2)
Unaware vasectomy still exists / exists at all	-	50.0 (1)	15.4 (2)	-	31.3 (5)
Husband's refusal (religious reasons cited for Muslims)	-	50.0 (1)	53.9 (7)	100.0 (1)	43.8 (7)
Want to take charge of birth control	100.0 (1)	-	-	-	-
Shy to tell husband about birth control	-	-	15.4 (2)	-	12.5 (2)
Total* (n)	100.0 (1)	100.0 (2)	100.0 (13)	100.0 (1)	100.0 (16)

* Excludes 3 households where neither spouse were engaged in paid work at the time of the survey.

Also, half of the Muslim wives had to accept their husbands' refusals (arguments mainly based on religious decree). In the remaining income allocation groups (C, D and E) there is a clear dichotomy in the views of Hindu and Muslim wives.

A majority of Hindu wives do not want to take the 'risks' of vasectomy in fear that their husbands would be incapacitated to continue providing for the household. For a majority of Muslim wives, the pervasive reason being that husbands refuse to obtain vasectomy on grounds of religious decree.

THE BIRTH CONTROL DECISION

For the majority of women in the sample, contraceptive options, if they exist at all, tend to be female-centric.

Table 5.8 Contraceptive Negotiations by Income Allocation Groups

	Group A Wife contributes > 40% Husband stable provider	Group B Wife contributes > 40% Husband unstable provider	Group C Wife contributes < 40% Husband stable provider	Group D Wife's money not used for household expenses Husband gives allowance	Group E Wife does not earn Husband gives allowance
Joint decision	83.3 (5)	13.6 (3)	11.5 (3)	20.0 (1)	5.3 (2)
Maintain secrecy with husband regarding birth control decisions	-	27.3 (6)	3.9 (1)	20.0 (1)	2.6 (1)
Openly go against husband's preferences	-	9.1 (2)	11.5 (3)	-	2.6 (1)
Husband provider, therefore cannot go against his wish	-	13.6 (3)	42.3 (11)	40.0 (2)	71.1 (27)
Part dependent on husband's per- mission, part abide by own decision	-	13.6 (3)	23.1 (6)	-	5.3 (2)
Never discuss birth control with husband	16.7 (1)	22.7 (5)	7.8 (2)	20.0 (1)	13.2 (5)
Total (n)	100.0 (6)	100.0 (22)	100.0 (26)	100.0 (5)	100.0 (38)

How do women settle for the birth control choices they make or want to make? What kind of negotiations do they engage in with their husbands[6] while opting for contraception?[7] Does the nature of arbitration differ across income-allocation groups in the pooling continuum and housekeeping allowance sets? These issues are explored in the ensuing section. Findings pertinent to religion, age, phase of family cycle, household structure (nuclear/extended) and number of living children are to be taken as similar unless otherwise indicated.

GROUP A

In Table 5.8, the majority (83.3%, five out of six wives) in this subgroup are able to tell their husbands what they want with regard to birth control. Thus, the spouses make a joint decision.

Recall (from Chapters 3 and 4) that a majority of the women in this group also have more egalitarian relations with their husbands and control over family decisions and income. Also, this is the only subgroup in which a majority of wives have some control over their bodies during sexual intercourse, in that their husbands do not force them into intercourse against their wish. The pattern of relative control continues when it comes to making birth control choices. To some extent, therefore, higher monetary contribution in the households and lesser income gaps with the husband are linked to wives' autonomy in birth control decision-making.

Aggregate trends, however, hide individual variations as Molina's case seems to indicate. Molina, the only wife in this subgroup who did not discuss her contraceptive choice with her husband is in the adult phase of family cycle, with four living children. She had obtained sterilization and did not resort to any non-terminal birth control prior to sterilization. Molina did not think it was 'proper' to discuss birth control with her husband since it was a 'female thing' (*meyeli byapar*). Thus, when she thought it was time for her to terminate her pregnancy, she went to the local health center, had the operation and then told her husband that she would not have any more children.

GROUP B

The nature of negotiations regarding birth control choice in this subgroup reflects the conflictual underpinnings of conjugal relationships in a majority of these households. Only three of the twenty-two wives said that they could jointly negotiate contraception with their husbands. Many (27.3%) kept secret their sterilization or any non-terminal (mostly pills) methods they had obtained.

This was, incidentally, true of Annapurna. In some instances, when husbands found out they threw away the pills and/or physically and verbally abused their wives:

> 'Now that you are earning, you think you can get all these things [meaning contraception] and sleep with other men!'

Almost a quarter of the women did not discuss birth control matters with their husbands. More than notions of 'proper' wifely behaviour, this pattern reflects absence of communication between spouses in this subgroup. Tripti refers to this situation as follows:

> 'He doesn't really care if I have two children or twenty. I know if he had his way he would have as many children as the number of bells in an anklet (*ghungroor moto bachcha banabay*)! So I never discuss birth control with him. I know that I have to earn and feed my family. So I went ahead and did what I wanted. Whether he knows or not, likes it or not, is not my headache.'

Recall (from Chapter 4) that husbands of half of the wives in this group apply force or threat to persuade wives to have sexual intercourse. The struggles that the wives go through to ward off undesired sexual propositions is once again reflected in their secret ventures and lone decisions at the time of contraceptive choice.

Women's covert strategies in obtaining birth control are apparent in studies of both industrialized and developing societies. In Pollack's study (1985) of the contraceptive careers of fifty, mostly white middle class British women attending graduate courses at university, he found that nearly all of the women preferred to take precautions rather than rely on partners. Morakvasic (1981:408) interviewed 258 migrant Yugoslav women who were wage labourers in Western Europe. These women considered abortion as the only viable method of birth control since use of other forms of birth control made them less sexually desirable to men. Again, their sexuality and capacity to bear children are closely related. In this instance, abortion is virtually *the* fertility control method since it leaves open the possibility for them to have sex and provide occasional proof of their fecundity to men. Consequently, Yugoslav women manage to have only the number of children they want. But their pregnancies are by no means planned since they lack sexual autonomy.

In a study conducted in Bangladesh, Kabeer (1985) shows that when conflicts arise between the wishes of landless Muslim women and those of other dominant members in the family, women may still exercise covert influence over the final outcome of reproductive behaviour. In Kabeer's sample women were using contraceptives without their husbands' knowledge since it was against their interests to have children. Ahmad and Zeidenstein (1982) found similar occurrences of covert contraceptive usage among Bangladeshi women in their village study sample. Poffenberger and Poffenberger (1973) observed that women in their sample found ways to avoid coitus and delay pregnancies by staying away from their husbands and sleeping with the children at night. Also, in the absence of proper contraceptive choices they took herbal pills from the village priest to avoid pregnancy. These instances are in many ways related to the experiences of wives in the sample. Currently, Bangladesh's Total Fertility Rate (TFR) has decreased drastically and is even lower than that of India (3.2 as opposed to 3.7 in India). Studies, however, still need to assess the processes through which this has been achieved in order to gauge the dynamics of the strategies adopted by women to achieve these ends.

GROUP C

The limits of wives' renegotiation is best reflected in this subgroup. Of course, most (42.3%) of the wives have to acquiesce to their husbands' wishes when it comes to making any birth control choice. In these instances, higher income give husbands the opportunity to exercise ultimate veto power. Almost a quarter of the women in the sample are partly dependent on their husbands' permission and partly abide by their own decision. In these cases wives try to exert covert control over some of their birth control choices while certain aspects of their decision-making are still controlled by their husbands. Bilkis's case illustrates the point.

Bilkis is a self-employed (Muslim) mother of four living children whose husband, a high-school graduate, contributes most of the income for the household. In her twenty years of marriage, she has had eight pregnancies, including four miscarriages. At the time of the interview Bilkis had already obtained a sterilization. Her sterilization, however, was completely contingent upon her husband's approval and she had to struggle for a long time to make him agree to the operation. Her husband's reluctance was mostly based on religious negations (apparently the reason why even he had refused to obtain vasectomy) coupled with the assertion, 'If I can feed the children, why do you [Bilkis] have to worry about having them?' 'So if I stopped having children my husband would feel that I am insulting him,' Bilkis explained. She continued, 'But I am a working woman and a mother. I know what it takes to run a family and I could not go on like this. So without telling him I started taking Mala [government distributed birth control pill].' Bilkis had to discontinue the pills since she started feeling very weak. Thus, she felt she had no other option but to terminate childbearing even though it was a sin (*gunah*) and she was very nervous about the decision. This step was more crucial than taking birth control pills partly because of the existing religious ban and also because her husband would be angry and hurt. He did not really want Bilkis to stop having children. Thus, 'I had to tell my guardian [husband] about this decision.' Months of coaxing, cajoling and negotiations with the husband followed. 'I know you bring in the money, but I have to work too. If I become weak like this, it is not good either,' Bilkis told her husband. The husband refused. Ultimately, the doctor had to intervene. She told Bilkis's husband that if he wanted his wife alive, he should either allow her sterilization or go for a sterilization himself. Exclaims Bilkis, 'That put some sense into his head; he finally permitted me to have the operation!' Bilkis's case is a cogent example of wives trying to redefine the outlines of their gender domains through avenues of paid work while still cowering to the ideological and material underpinnings of their husbands' superior position in the household.

GROUPS D AND E

Birth control negotiations of wives in these two subgroups followed the predictable pattern. Given that wives' income do not contribute to household expenditures, while husbands' incomes do, most wives (40 percent in Group D and 71.1 percent in Group E) took a more passive stance in birth control negotiations. The wives felt that they could not overstep their boundaries by taking any contraceptive decision that their husbands did not agree to. Kakoli expressed her exasperation at this situation in this manner:

> 'What can I do? We are women. We take all the initiatives but if men don't listen there is nothing we can do because they are our guardians, they bring in the money. Women keep getting pregnant because of men. Too many babies come, because of men. You go near them and you get pregnant.'

Kakoli's comment typifies the women's realizations about the limitations of their gender, given their household situations. Recall (from Chapter 4) that the husbands of most women in these groups are also able to either apply force or threat of force/desertion to induce their wives to have intercourse. Moreover, some wives, apprehensive about displeasing their husbands do not even verbalize their wish against having sexual intercourse. Kakoli's view reinstates once more the nature of women's limited control over their bodies during intercourse. In fact, at different points during their interviews, 42 percent of the women equated 'going near the husband' to pregnancy. Further, the husband's economic contribution puts substantial constraints on the reproductive prerogatives of wives in both groups in the housekeeping allowance set in general and in the group where wives are not engaged in remunerative work while husbands give household allowance, in particular.

Cognizance of this constraint becomes evident in Rameswari's situation in an extended household in the early phase of family cycle:

> 'I got pregnant very soon after marriage. My mother-in-law said, "That's a shame, what will people say. Go get an abortion." I said all right. My mother-in-law told my child's father what she told me. He said, "No, I will feed my children." So I had the baby. What can I say. I am not the one who works around here. I feel that if the person who brings the food for the household is wishing something, I cannot say anything over and above that or go against his wish.'

Overall, for a majority of the wives who receive allowances from their husbands (Groups D and E), birth control selection has to be accommodated within the larger framework of their household situations characterized by dependence upon husbands for one's own and the family's well-being.

Thus, the exploration of the dynamics of wives' birth control trajectories reveal the constraints within which they struggle for reproductive control. The consistent pattern of female sterilization evinced in the sample indicates that most of the wives have to ultimately rely upon female-centred terminal methods of birth control. Besides the negative consequences female sterilization might have in terms of women's health and population growth (Chatterjee 1989; Basu 1985; Mathur and Sharma 1995), it puts almost the entire responsibility of birth control upon women. Although, it is true that female sterilization services are preferable to no family planning services at all, the findings in this chapter raise questions about the actual choice women have in selecting birth control at both societal and household levels.

Feminist critiques of India's family planning services have repeatedly asserted that in the Indian context, female sterilization is not an indicator of innovative and voluntary method choice for women (while usage of non-terminal methods is) since several external factors like programme options and lack of information and effectiveness may channel women's selection towards female sterilization instead of other non-terminal birth control methods (Basu 1984; 1985; 1992; Basu and Sundar 1988).

In this sample, a majority (58%) had never used any non-terminal method of birth control. Of the 42 women who practiced some non-terminal method (including rhythm, withdrawal and abstinence), 19 obtained sterilization because either lack of cooperation of husbands or problems and failures of the non-terminal methods used, impelled them to do so. The majority of those remaining had to abandon the non-terminal methods they were using for similar reasons. Only five women were using and continuing with non-terminal methods at the time of the survey. Thus, female sterilization seems to be a 'choice' stemming from lack of other options, ignorance, inefficacy and inconveniences of using other methods.

Women's views and experiences with male sterilization (vasectomy) further reiterates this point. It is indeed striking that since the Emergency in India in 1976 (when the vasectomy rate reached its peak), none of the husbands had obtained a vasectomy, despite the fact that it remains a prominent method in the Family Planning Programme agenda. Ignorance and misinformation still cloud women's knowledge of vasectomy. So much so that more than a quarter (29%) of the women were not even aware that male sterilization (vasectomy) existed at all. Thus, at least for the women in this study, the Family Planning Programme has been unsuccessful in addressing the ignorance and fear of vasectomy procedures. Further, husbands do not undermine or dispel their wives' notions by obtaining vasectomies.

Besides ignorance and misinformation, responses relating to absence of vasectomy and consequent emphasis on female sterilization seem to show that the women's intra-household income allocation and gender situations are also critically linked to their perceptions about and practice of birth control. The historical processes of class and gender formation and their articulations in the women's lives give them minimal spaces within which to exert fertility control. In some cases, the husband's paid work and greater economic contribution in the household in relation to the wife's generates the notion that the responsibility of 'risking' sterilization must be borne by wives and not by husbands since, apparently, a household can survive without a woman, but not without a man. This view is expressed by a majority of the wives even when they contribute more than 40 percent of the household expenses.

In Muslim households, a majority of the husbands are able to refuse to obtain a vasectomy on religious grounds (and absolve themselves from committing a sin). Wives not only accept the refusals but in half of the cases, they actually obtain sterilization themselves at considerable psychological cost. Perhaps, the acceptance of the husbands' refusal and gender-differentiated double standards in obtaining sterilization is linked to the fact that a majority of the husbands are, once again, the main economic providers. Comparison of responses of Hindu and Muslim wives in this context reveals an interesting situation. A majority of Hindu wives feel that it is better for women to get sterilized since husbands should not risk sterilization because of their higher earning potential. Consequently, when possible, these wives obtain sterilization themselves. The religious ban creates a more difficult sterilization decision-making scenario for Muslim wives. First, a majority of them have to accept their husbands' refusal to undergo vasectomy based on religious prohibition. Consequently, many of them obtain sterilization themselves, but not without undergoing feelings of guilt and stress at the fact that they have gone against the religious dictum. This scenario might prolong the decision-making process and actual procurement of sterilization for these wives. One wonders if the fact that Muslim wives have a higher number of pregnancies (and living children) than Hindu wives is linked to this longer period of weighing the consequences of sterilization.

The limits of the wives' struggles in birth control decisions and their links to differential spousal income contribution becomes more evident in the nature of negotiations the women employ in matters related to contraception. The majority of wives in Group A are able to discuss their birth control preferences and desires openly with their husbands. Recall, however, that 60 percent of these wives feel that husbands being the main income earners should not be allowed to risk sterilization. So the ideological and material underpinnings of husband's superior position in the household still prevail among this group.

In other income-allocation groups, a majority of the wives cannot be candid about their opinions regarding birth control. A wife's arbitration ranges from secrecy to conforming to her husband's birth control preferences. In cases where wives contribute less than 40 percent of household expenses or they do not contribute at all, husbands clearly have the upper hand in making birth control decisions. These wives openly express that their husbands' income contribution prevents them from going against their husbands' wishes in matters relating to birth control. But in cases where the wives contribute more than 40 percent of household expenses and the husbands have either stopped contributing or contribute irregularly (Group B), a majority of the wives still have to adopt covert techniques to implement their birth control decisions.

The main income-provider status does not give them the right to express their preferences as openly as it does for the main income-provider husbands in the former subgroups. At an absolute level, then, paid work and contribution to household expenses does not seem to significantly alleviate the wives' positions.

Relatively, however, we find that modal and majority groups of the wives contributing more than 40 percent of household expenses (Groups A and B) can express some agency in birth control negotiations (however conflictual the process might be) to attain their objectives. Significantly, the husbands do not exert ultimate veto power in birth control decisions in either of these groups. Thus, however asymmetric the conjugal exchanges might seem to an outsider, a majority of the women with higher contribution into the household pool can at least adopt some overt or covert strategies to obtain birth control.

Thus, family planning services made available to the women seem to capitalize upon their class and gender situations and work within their subordination at a societal level. At another level, aspects of the wives' gender articulation and nature of material exchanges in the household seem to be linked to their perceptions, practice and negotiations on to birth control. This, too, serves to undermine their position and perpetuate their subordination as a gender within the working class.

NOTES

1. See Question 71 in the Appendix. Respondents talked of their constraints, obligations, nature of negotiations with husband, kin and future plans in response to these questions.
2. Number of the Muslim women viewed sterilization as against Islam and therefore, a sin (gunah). The sterilized person would have to suffer far reaching consequences — she/he would not be honoured by the community after death; no one would carry his/her pall, read the prayer or put soil on his/her grave.
3. Since this group does not contain any Muslim women none of them is forbidden by religion to obtain sterilization. They were not thinking of sterilization at the time because they wanted to have children first.
4. Consequently, the high incidence of unprotected couples in the sample is a sad commentary on the inadequacies of contraceptive technology in general and performance of the government's family planning programme (in terms of creating contraceptive awareness, fulfilling unmet contraceptive needs and securing women's reproductive prerogatives), in particular. Although West Bengal government's per capita expenditure on health and 'Family Welfare' (implying birth control provisions) has approximately doubled and become six times as much respectively, between 1980-81 and 1989-90 (*Health on the March* 1992: Table V.3), the high incidence of 'unprotected' couples in the sample does not reflect favorably on the performance of the government's programme. Couple Protection Rate (CPR) in West Ben-

gal in 1996-97 is 37.6 and the per capita expenditure on health is Rs 69.65 and on family welfare is Rs 12.07 in 1995-96 (*Health on the March* 1996-97).

5. Regarding the link between contraceptive use and spousal dynamics, a majority (56.5%) of women who were not practising any form of birth control reported that their husbands either did not care about limiting family size or would not hear of contraception until they had one or two sons (20% of the cases). Of these women, more than half (53.9%) reported not being able to go against their husbands' wishes in matters related to contraceptive use. Clearly, therefore, husbands' domination prevented many women in the sample from obtaining any form of birth control.
6. The variable measuring conjugal negotiations in birth control matters is computed through content analysis of responses to two questions related to women's control over acquiring any method of birth control.
7. The focus here is mainly on women's negotiations with their husbands since for a majority of women, these negotiations formed the crux of their struggle to control their fertility. However, some women were engaged in simultaneous birth control negotiations with their marital kin who might want their daughters-in-law to have a son and consequently, disallow contraception. Again, a couple of Muslim women had to keep their sterilization a secret from the community and religious heads. All these factors added to the complexity of the wives' struggle.

CONCLUSION

This exploration of the sexual histories of slum-dwelling women in has brought to light some of the linkages between intra-household dynamics and the articulation of choices of poor working class women in the sexual and birth control domains. Using the theoretical rubric of Gender and Development (GAD), I aimed to arrive at a holistic understanding of women's experiences and actions in these aspects of their lives, and to evaluate their implications in terms of gender formation in the working class. At a general level, the research has succeeded in uncovering some of the crucial links between the material basis of household formation of gender and the intimate interactions related to sexual and birth control decision-making. More specifically, key issues raised are summarized along several dimensions.

One of the primary concerns in this research was to focus on processes related to reproduction instead of outcomes of reproduction per se. Examining only quantifiable elements like number of children or use of birth control does not necessarily render a full picture of women's control over their generative capacities and sexual lives. Rather, as the findings in Chapters 4 and 5 show, one has also to understand the circumstances within which women's reproductive decisions take shape. Development policies pertaining to population control are, for the most part, blind to the intricacies of poor women's circumstances. Family planning programmes tend to objectify women as 'clients'. In the process, women's daily struggles for survival as wives, mothers, sexual partners, income-earners and home-makers and so on are overlooked. Consequently, family planning programmes introduce and popularize female-centred, terminal and outcome-oriented birth control methods which do not ultimately help to alleviate the situation of women or contain population growth. Rather, in some instance, they serve to perpetuate women's gender subordination (see Chapter 4). That is why a focus on process, rather than outcomes is crucial. Two areas elemental in processes leading to reproductive outcomes were explored. These relate to women's sexual and birth control negotiations with their husbands. Brief descriptions of the findings are in order.

Delineation of sexual encounters, attitudes and behaviours evident in Chapter 4 elucidate that expression of women's sexuality and sexual interests may be separate and distinct from that of their husbands. Moreover, the conjugal dynamics during intercourse and negotiations pertaining to birth control suggest that women's birth control choices (or lack thereof) may not necessarily reflect decisions of a 'couple'. In fact, patterns of differential conjugal dynamics during intercourse question certain assumptions of mainstream demographic research. The latter postulates data collection on ovulation, fecundity, coital frequency and risk of conception (for couples without contraceptives) for family planning programme management (Blanc and Rutenberg 1991; Chaudhury 1990; Dixon-Mueller 1996), treating these factors as objective biological and physical phenomena. The presumption is that knowledge of ovulation intervals, fecund periods, frequency of coitus, unprotected 'eligible' couples (wife and husband within 15 to 45 years of age) will adequately help shape planned contraceptive intervention through family planning programmes to limit family size.

Explorations show that there may be certain underlying gender dynamics and material realities of household situations which undermine these simplistic approaches and solutions forwarded by family planning research and policy, however. Indeed, there appear to be links between the husband's forceful dominance in the sexual domain and his power wielding in contraceptive decision-making. Thus, irrespective of when a wife ovulates, or when she is fecund, or when a 'couple' is under risk of conception, the politics of sex and birth control negotiations and bargaining will most likely, perhaps invariably, influence biology. In other words, there will always be separateness of spousal domains and differential conjugal autonomy within households, which may belie policy interventions based on 'biological' data (Dixon-Mueller 1996). Unless mainstream demographic research and policy are able to address these issues and explore the intra-household dynamics of gender and resource allocation and asymmetrical conjugal reciprocities, the baffling mystery of population growth may never be solved.

What does the exploration of sexual and birth control negotiations reveal in terms of women's position as a gender? First, there are indications (see Chapter 4) that ideological, material and coercive factors limit women's control over their bodies during sexual interaction and satisfaction after sexual interactions with husbands. Additionally (see Chapter 5), women may have no say against their husbands decisions regarding birth control; or they may have to exercise covert techniques at considerable risks to attain their birth control objectives.

Why do women accept these seemingly asymmetrical exchanges in the sexual and birth control domains? To some extent, of course, ideology plays a decisive role. Recall the submissive prototype of Indian wifehood, which is still relevant (Poffenberger and Poffenberger 1973), and dominant cultural underpinnings of Indian women's passive sexuality and male aggressiveness. Manifestations of these ideals abound throughout the study: in some women's inclination to consider their husbands guardian of the household despite being the main income-earners or, in some women's reluctance to initiate sex because 'a woman is not supposed to ask for it' and so on. But ideology is definitely not the only factor which comes into play. As the exploration of the linkages in Chapters 4 and 5 showed, a woman's dependence on her husband for economic sustenance of herself and her children possibly increases the likelihood of her passivity in sexual and birth control negotiations. In these instances, then, a woman's passivity can be interpreted not merely as an ideological syndrome but also a strategy to secure her own and her family's well-being within the minimum spaces of control available to her. To date, there seems to have been little or no data in India pertaining to the links between poor women's socioeconomic position in the household and the nature of sexual autonomy. This book explores these uncharted domains revealing in the process how women's sexual agency may be intricately linked to her material position and gender in relation to her husband.

I found women whose sexual lives are filled with conflicts and conformity and sexual confrontations typified by force and threat at the end of sixteen-hour work days. There were women who had to deal with suspicious husbands after acquiring birth control. Some other women obtained sterilization because they felt that loss of their lives (if the sterilization operation turned fatal) would make little difference to the well-being of their households while that of their husbands would. To the extent that these experiences form the realities of a majority of women's lives in the study, it may be said that the processes influencing and emerging from the women's sexual and birth control experiences serve to perpetuate and reinforce women's subordination as a gender and class. Of course, one cannot discount the women's struggles at carving out niches for sexual and birth control agency. Thus focusing on processes irrespective of fertility outcomes facilitates more tangible, holistic and humanistic analysis of women's experiences and actions and their societal implications. Also, it points to the significance of treating women as sexual, reproductive and thinking human beings instead of mere vehicles of reproduction.

The curtain is yet to fall on the ongoing debate on the role of income in empowering poor Third World women. While this book does not propose any definitive conclusion to this debate, it does reveal that patterns of income pooling and housekeeping allowance remittal are crucially related to women's control over household income and resources and, consequently, their sexual and birth control decision-making. Beneria and Roldan (1987) have come up with findings that are similar: ideals of husband's superiority seem to play a crucial role in influencing this outcome.

Material and coercive factors also influence perpetuation of material and gender differentials between spouses in the household. As findings in Chapter 2 seem to suggest, one of the reasons behind this may be that in the historical processes of class and gender formation, women's access to societal resources like education and income may be invariably constrained by the limits of their gender. Manifestations of these gender-based differentials are evident even in the small non-random sample of one hundred women in this study. Women have lesser years of education than their husbands and invariably earn less than their husbands. Additionally, while more husbands work in the organized (proletarian) sectors, all wives are in unorganized (subproletarian) sector occupations. Even within the unorganized sectors more husbands are in relatively more stable, secure and high wage occupations than wives.

These gender-based class differences may be seen as forming some of the basis of the divergence in resource contribution and control between husbands and wives within the household. Consequently, most husbands who pool incomes have full or partial prerogatives to spend money on themselves and, in the process, control and regulate money flow within the household. All wives pooling their incomes cannot afford this prerogative. Moreover, wives not earning any income are completely dependent upon their husband's contributions. As we saw, these trends can be further compounded by ideological underpinnings and coercion by the husband.

Overall, it seems clear that paid work may not be the panacea to overcome working class women's subordination. The nature of a woman's agency from paid work may vary on the basis of her household circumstances, her position in the phase of family cycle or her husband's economic situation. To the extent that economic austerities throughout the Third World increasingly make paid work a reality for a majority of women and structural adjustments and privatization reduce government's investments in social progress, gender inequalities and impoverishment of women would perpetuate (Anand 1994). In this context the dynamics between women's economic contribution and household situation becomes a significant area of research.

One of the objectives of this exploration was to trace the creation and recreation of societal gender traits within the working class, through events unfolding in the women's lives, making it necessary to go back and forth through the fluid trajectories of a woman's life course. Exploration of some of the women's childhood events in the premarriage phase of their lives showed that within the working class growing up in economically stable households (proletarian, informal sector, petty bourgeoisie), rather than economically unstable ones (subproletarian), might give women greater opportunities for education (Chapter 2). But as we saw in the case of the respondents, these benefits may be undermined on the basis of gender. The differential educational and domestic work experiences of women compared to their brothers and the termination or absence of educational training for reasons typically ascribed to a girl's gender are coupled with the similarity of women's life-chances conditioned by dynamics of gender. Moreover, within the marital household, differences in husbands and wives manifested through contrasting occupations and incomes, household division of labour, sexual prerogatives and birth control experiences seem to influence the reproduction and recomposition of a working class separated across gender.

Additionally, the women's location in Calcutta places them in a labour market known to be segregated on the basis of gender with the benefits pertaining to availability and accessibility of occupations and wages accruing to men (N. Banerjee 1985; 1991; N. Banerjee and Mitter 1998). The occupational and income trajectories of women in the sample compared to their husbands make this reasonably evident. Also, we saw how availability and selection of birth control methods which put the onus of terminal birth control on the majority of the women in the sample (Chapter 5) may be circumscribed by methods promoted and popularized by the government's family planning programme instead of women's informed choices. Overall, the dialectical combination of these intra- and extra-household elements affecting lives of working class women in poverty may be associated with the social reproduction of women's subordination as a gender.

Accepting that this case study is based on a small non-random sample and the linkages revealed are outcomes of an exploratory exercise, this analysis nevertheless makes some significant contributions in the realm of intra-household research in India, particularly those pertaining to women in poverty. Over the past two decades, socialist feminist scholarship in India has asserted the need to focus on gender and material resource-based dynamics within the household, to expose the 'power dimensions of household structures that affect the allocation of labour, time and other resources within the family' (Mazumdar and Sharma 1990: 186; A. Sen 1995). The methodology applied to decompose the household unit in this study (adapted from Beneria and Roldan 1987) helps reveal intra-household power structures expressed through income allocation and control, phase of family life cycles and division of household labour. The strategy also helps to uncover some of the material basis of household formation of gender differentials within a particular class and its linkages with intimate domains of sexual and birth control experiences of women. Moreover, a concerted effort is made to treat the women as subjects instead of objectifying them as cases. This is coupled with an attempt to evaluate experiences from women's own perspectives and to understand the fluid trajectories of their class and gender experiences spanning their pre-and post-marital lives. This approach renders a better understanding of the household contexts within which the women act and the unfolding processes of societal class and gender formation. Future research can gain from this methodological contribution.

The theoretical framework of Gender and Development facilitates analysis of the process of development at a holistic level. Also, it questions the institutionalized assumptions upon which current development policies are based. In the process, the Gender and Development framework helps to promote comparative research pertaining to the world's women (Parpart 1989; G. Sen and Grown 1987; Correa and Reichman 1994). However, the theory does not lend itself easily to policy prescriptions in ongoing development strategies and programmes (Rathgeber 1990). Working within this perspective, I was able to uncover some of the complexities that characterize poor women's household situations. It was possible to recognize some of the forces leading to and reproducing contours of women's societal subordination and the paradoxes of poor women's realities as they try to balance the ideological and material. Additionally, the exercise also exposed how long- and short-term gender interests of working class women may not necessarily conform to abstract ideals of feminist emancipation. But it becomes difficult to channel these findings 'into viable, broad-based societal development plans and programmes' (ibid.: 495).

It does not seem fair to elucidate and analyse the women's situations without suggesting any solutions to the insurmountable problems they face in their struggles for daily survival. The constraints of policy formulation in Gender and Development only show that there may be no concrete long- or short-term solutions to all the problems in women's lives revealed in the analysis. Nothing short of overhauling extant structures of class and gender formation can make that happen. Some tangible and relatively workable solutions, however, are in order. At a general level, while giving women more income-earning opportunities and facilitating their mobility in the organized sector is desirable, immediate improvement of the growing number of poor working women's situations in Calcutta lies in organizing their occupations within the 'unorganized' (informal) sector. Moreover, giving women more educational opportunities is essential, but not without creating awareness about the necessity to educate girls and deemphasizing the significance of early marriage through media and Non-Governmental Organizations.

Specially, in matters related to birth control, some solutions are imperative. While conducting the interviews I came across numerous women asking me about viable contraception, 'one that works like magic!', as one woman put it. Every time I completed an interview, I came back with the frustrating conviction that the government's family planning programme has failed. Of course, more hazard-free contraceptive techniques for both men and women will ultimately resolve the crisis. But some immediate steps need to be taken. All along, the approach of the family planning programme has been to set up outlets for obtaining birth control. It is assumed that 'clients' requiring contraceptive protection will approach these outlets. This strategy has not materialized in practice. The programme has only a few choices to offer and it emphasizes particular forms of contraception in relation to others. Moreover, the basic structure of the programme remains the same in that men and women mostly need to obtain birth control from these outlets. Of course, there is the occasional health worker who visits households, rarely following up or monitoring the birth control obtained. At least, this was the experience of women in the sample who were visited by health workers. Besides, even a cursory glance at the family planning budgets will show (for instance, West Bengal's health budget) that the majority of expenses incurred by the government are on infrastructure items like buildings, sterilization beds, advertisements and automobiles (*Health on the March* 1996-97).

This approach requires alteration. It will be much more pragmatic to form small networks where trained social workers assigned to groups of wives and husbands can discuss, educate, inform and elucidate upon and supply extant birth control methods. The immediate need is to de-emphasize the insistence on female sterilization, educate men and women about vasectomy and generate an awareness of non-terminal birth control methods (Basu 1986; Barnett and Stein 1998).

Of course, given the constraints upon women's time, scheduling regular meetings may be problematic. Additionally, strained conjugal relations may make it quite impossible to have both spouses present. Notwithstanding these factors, a social worker's interaction with small groups will facilitate sensitization of poor women's specific household situations, understanding of which is absolutely imperative to help secure reproductive prerogatives of women (and men).

Various prospects for future research emerge: First, the effects of intra-household dynamics of sexual and birth control negotiations on family size and desired sex of children can be examined as a next step towards understanding the facets of poor women's reproductive decision-making processes. Again, although the case study methodology provided a contextual focus on a group of women's lives, some limitations of cross-sectional data collection became evident in the process. For instance, women's negotiations about birth control may have taken place at different junctions of their marital life-course. However, when I discussed the issue within the household context, the assumption being made was that a similar structure prevailed when the actual birth control negotiations took place. A similar problem was encountered with relation to women's paid work-status. Many women, who were clearly only temporarily out of paid work, had to be coded as one in the housekeeping allowance set when in reality they may well have been in different income allocation categories as the trajectories of their sexual and birth control experiences evolved. Overall, it seems that cross-sectional data analysis is not adequately equipped to capture the fluidity of subjects' life-situations. These limitations call for a longitudinal analysis which is able to establish the time sequence of events. It would be worthwhile to follow a group of, say, 50 women from their older childhood up to the termination of their childbearing years and engage in an exploration similar to the present study. Finally, the linkages revealed in this research need to be tested on a larger and randomly selected sample.

In one of the first slums I visited during the survey, I met a women who asked me what good this study would do. 'You will get what you want out of it,' she said, 'while we will keep struggling the way we have been doing all our lives. Nothing will change.'I only hope that her prediction is not entirely true.

AFTERWORD

The opportunity I had to elicit oral histories from a range of vibrant women was, in itself, a rich learning experience, one that continues to influence my life today. I have come to this realization more and more as my own life has changed drastically from what it was four years ago when I undertook the research. Then, I was a student—a nervous graduate tying up the loose ends of a dissertation into a neat 'defendable' knot that would please my advisor and committee members well enough to make them grant me a Ph.D. The trials and tribulations of these women seemed a distant event. Now, as a wife and a mother settled in Calcutta with a full-time job and an extended family, every moment of my life, I find myself involved in the precarious balancing act which was so much a part of the lives of the hundred-odd women I have talked about throughout this book. The fact that despite the best of intentions and a wellspring of support from family, friends and colleagues, it has taken me a very long time to work on this book is itself indicative of the difficulties I have faced in making choices and setting priorities within my own gendered household context. Now, more than ever before, I feel an invisible bond of sisterhood with the women I met.

I can clearly hear Rezwana's voice saying:

> 'Days go by and nights go by and I have to be everywhere all the time cooking, washing, feeding my children, taking my mother-in-law to the doctor, talking to my husband—and this is what we have to do—because we are women. How can we think of ourselves? There are so many others who need us.'

In the four years that I have worked in Calcutta—first, in the Women's Studies Department of Calcutta University and then, in the social research divisions of two consultancy agencies—I have attended scores of feminist workshops, and met with the under secretaries of various government departments, representatives of NGOs, international agencies and the corporate sector. Every time we discuss the problems of impoverished women, the emphasis is on the specific programme funded. The associated ramifications are largely ignored. When we are discussing sexual health, we focus on STD/HIV but overlook the issue of emergency obstetric care. When we are discussing displacement of families because of, for instance, a coal project, we focus on women's vocational training needs but not on the social consequences of rehabilitation such as the greater likelihood of alcoholism and violence of the men in their families whose earnings would increase with the coming of a coal mine. This is how funded programmes operationalize 'development' in our country and, presumably, on all corners of the Third World: in segmented compartments of funded programmes. We talk about linkages and networking in our ivory tower workshops in airconditioned seminar rooms, but in reality how much linkage have we been able to generate?

I met Sarju about a year ago when I was visiting the slum she lives in while working on a water-sanitation project. Her daughter could not be sent to school since, 'she is now grown up enough to cook and my husband does not want to cook anymore.' Her husband seems more frail but his wife-beatings continue as before. He reprimands her if she cannot provide for his daily five-rupee quota of alcohol. A more cynical Sarju has not felt the urge to network with other women to discuss the problem of violence she faces within the family. Nor have any of the many women's groups working in the city today networked with her to help her sort things out.

Annapurna is still working in our house doing part time chores. She, and thousands of others from her slum, were bulldozed out one night to make way for a road which was to be built over their homes before the coming festival season. Her husband is now living with her, having deserted his second wife after burdening her with two children. He works off and on at his carpentry job. The family has now moved to a village in the south of West Bengal where Annapurna had bought a piece of land some years ago from her own savings There is no job for her in the village and her husband's income is still not stable, though he earns more than her when he *does* get work. Her two boys are going to a government school and her daughter, who is the eldest, has just completed Class 10.

In order to manage her family, Annapurna catches the 4 a.m. train to the city, washes dishes and wipes floors in four middle class households and returns to her home at the end of the day. Her sister told me about Annapurna's husband:

> 'He has become sober now . . . he only beats Annapurna when he is drunk. Of course, it is a relief that she will not become pregnant any more—at least she can bring up her children. But again, my sister is very often upset since she underwent sterilization because my brother-in-law keeps doubting her. He says, "Now that you can't have children any more you can do whatever you want [implying, be unfaithful with other men]! Why do you have to go to the city to do your job—you think you can fool me?"'

Not much has changed for Annapurna but there is hope that her young daughter may—in a small way—transform a vicious circle of poverty, limited education and employment into a virtuous one.

Have we ever thought about what a woman like Annapurna has to encounter within her household even after she has publicly demonstrated the strength to buy her own piece of land and access sterilization facilities, the only viable method of contraception available to her?

The Gender and Development Theory has surely recognized the grey areas which shape the contours of women's struggles at work and at home. But in practice, at least within the domains of the women's movement in Calcutta, these issues have not been addressed and even if they have been, their scope is limited. The main reason for this abysmal lack of progress is that while focusing on issues of women, activists, practitioners and policy implementers have largely ignored men. In reality, of course, as we have seen throughout this book, men have played critical roles in defining the milieus of the women's lives. Consequently, we need to start thinking about interventions that would enable men to shift the paradigms of their thought processes—a difficult, perhaps, even utopian task. The feminist movement cannot but address these issues.

The Reproductive Child Health Programme being introduced by the Indian government has created a ripple in the stagnant waters of past birth control practices. The programme, which is geared towards both men and women, focuses upon the entire gamut of reproductive tract infections, Sexually Transmitted Diseases and contraceptive delivery, rather than being limited merely to target-oriented contraceptive deliveries and sterilization. Also, at a policy level, the government has decided to do away with the target-oriented programme focus on birth control. The programme is still at the planning stage and the present infrastructure is not yet geared to this approach. These are small beginnings. And it is for such beginnings that Annapurna and Sarju's children are waiting.

Calcutta, Oct 1999 A.S.

APPENDIX

QUESTIONNAIRE

SELECT QUESTIONS USED FOR ANALYSIS IN THE STUDY

I.D. # ____________

I WOULD LIKE TO BEGIN BY ASKING A FEW QUESTIONS ABOUT YOURSELF

1. Show me your ration card.
   (IF NOT IN POSSESSION OF ONE) How old are you ?
2. How old is your husband ?
3. How many children do you have ?
4. How many people live in your house/room ?
4a. Who are they ?
5. Where were you born ?
6. Where are your parents from ?
7a. Where was your husband born ?
7a. Where are his parents from ?
8. Where all have you lived since you were born ?
9. (For those not born in Calcutta)
   When did you first start living in Calcutta?
10. How long have you been living where you are now?

NOW A FEW THINGS ABOUT YOUR CHILDHOOD

11. What kind of work did your father normally do while you were growing up?
    (*Probe*: When respondent was less than ten or less/eleven to twelve years old)
12. What kind of work did your mother normally do while you were growing up?
    (*Probe: Who ran the family?)*
13. How many brothers and sisters do you have?
13a. How many are older than you?
13b. How many are younger than you?

14. From what you remember of your childhood, did you do any domestic work around the house? Describe.
15. Besides that did you work for money elsewhere?
15a. (If yes) What did you do with the money?
16. Did your sister/sisters do any domestic work around the house? Describe.
17. Did they work for wage?
17a. (If yes) What did they do with the money?
18. Did your brothers do any domestic work around the house? Describe.
19. Did they work for wage?
19a. (If yes) What did they do with the money?
20. Have you ever been to school? (before marriage)
20a. (If yes) How many years have you attended school?
20b. Why did you discontinue?
20c. (If never been to school) Why not?
21. Have you ever been taught at home? (before marriage)
21a. (If yes) For how many years?
22. Have you ever tried to study as an adult ?(after marriage)
22a. (If yes) How?
23. Can you sign your name?
24. Can you read numbers on buses?
25. Can you read a newspaper?
26. Can you write a letter?
27. What about your siblings: did your sister(s) go to school/study at home/with employer?
27a. (If yes) For how many years?
27b. (If no) Why
27c. Can she/they read a newspaper?
27d. Can she/they write a letter?
28. Did your brother(s) go to school/study at home/with employer
28a. (If yes) For how many years?
28b. (If no) Why?
28c. Can he/they read a newspaper?
28d. Can he/they write a letter?
29. Did your husband go to school/study at home/with employer?
29a. (If yes) For how many years?
29b. Can he read a newspaper?
29c. Can he write a letter?

A FEW QUESTIONS ABOUT THE WORK THAT YOU DO

30. Do you do remunerative work?
30a. (If no) Why not?
31. What kind of place do you work for?
(*Probe*: Domestic, sweat shops/type of wage/benefits)
32. What do they make or do?
33. What do you actually do in the job?
34. How many days a week do you work?
35. On a typical day what time do you begin work ? Can you give me a breakdown of your work hours on a typical day?
36. What time do you end work?
37. Currently how much do you earn at the end of the mouth/week/day?
38. What do you do with the money?
39. What kind of work does you husband do?
(*Probe*: type of wage/benefits and so on)
40. Is he working at the moment?
41. Currently how much money does your husband earn at the end of the month/week/day?
42. What does he do with the money?
43. Do you get money to run the family from anyone or anywhere else?
43a. (If yes) How much?
44. What is your monthly family income?
45. Do you have any personal savings?
(*Probe*: monthly/weekly/daily household expense)
45a. (If yes to savings) What are they?
(*Probe*: land, money in bank, jewellery-silver/gold/How much do you have?)

NOW ABOUT YOUR HOUSEWORK

46. On a typical day what is your schedule of housework?
47. Does your husband help with your housework?
47a. (If yes) How often?
47b. In what way? (Probe: go to the bazar, cook, look after child/children, fix things around house, pay bills)
48. Does anyone else help with your housework?
48a. (If yes) Who?
49. In what way?
50. On a typical day do you get time to relax?

50a. (If yes) What do you do then?
51. Do you get to chat with friends?
52. Do you get to watch TV?
52a. (If yes) How often? Where
53. Do you get to see cinemas in theatres?
53a. (If yes) How often? With whom?
54. Do you listen to the radio?
54a. (If yes) Where?
55. Do you ever go for outings with your husband/children say to the zoo, Victoria Memorial, Museum and so on?

NOW I WOULD LIKE TO KNOW ABOUT YOUR MARRIAGE

56. How many years have you been married?
57. Was this an arranged marriage or did you marry on your own?
58. How old were you when you married?
59. How many months after marriage did you conceive your first child?

NOW I WOULD LIKE TO ASK ABOUT YOUR CHILDREN

60. History of all pregnancies

age of child	how child died	visit doctor when pregnant	take medicine when pregnant	where child born

(Gather information on first up to tenth pregnancy)

61. Prior to marriage did the female elders in your family/friends ever tell you or did you know from any experience about how you should get intimate with your husband, how you get children and so on?

NOW I WOULD LIKE TO TALK TO YOU ABOUT YOUR FEELINGS CONCERNING FAMILY PLANNING

62. Do you know of/how (*Probe*: describe) have you (or husband) used
Tubectomy/Laparoscopy
Vasectomy
Abortion
Pill
Loop
Copper-T

Condom
Rhythm
Abstinence
Withdrawal
Why/Why not?
How did/would you go about it?

63. How many children do you think a woman should have before she stops having children altogether?
64. (If respondent is not practising any form of birth control) Do you think you should use any birth control methods?
65. (If respondent was not practising birth control at any point in her childbearing career) Why were you not using birth control methods at the time? (Specify time according to individual respondent.)
66. What does your husband feel about birth control?
67. Do you discuss matters relating to family planning, birth control and so on with your husband ? (If yes) How often do you discuss these matters ?

NOW I AM GOING TO ASK SOME QUESTIONS ABOUT YOUR PHYSICAL RELATIONSHIP WITH YOUR HUSBAND. THIS IS VERY IMPORTANT SINCE I WANT TO UNDERSTAND HOW FAMILIES MAKE DECISIONS THROUGH THEIR SEXUAL BEHAVIOURS.

68. How is love expressed between you and your husband? (*Probe* : Is it mental, physical or both?)
69. Do you sleep next to your husband at night? (*Probe* : where/how do the others sleep)
70. Do you feel tense during intercourse in the presence of others in the room?
71. When your husband wants to have sex with you how does he communicate this to you?
72. What happens when your husband wants to have sex and you don't feel like it
73. Do you ever initiate sex with your husband ? (If yes) How ? (if no) Why not
74. How often did you have intercourse in the past week/month
75. When intercourse is over how do you feel
76. Do you get to know how your husband feels?

NOW I HAVE A FEW QUESTIONS ABOUT YOUR FAMILY ENVIRONMENT

77. If you and your husband are purchasing something for the house, or buying clothes or food how do you go about it? Who makes the final decision?
78. Does your husband drink alcohol?
78a. (If yes) How frequently?
79. Are there any problems with drug use in your family? (if yes) With whom?
80. Does your husband get angry with you or your children?
81. Does he hit you or your children when he gets angry?
82. Has he ever threatened you with a knife or any other weapon?
83. Taking all things together, how do you feel about your family life?
(*Probe*: for specific experiences, descriptions, if she is optimistic/pessimistic about her children, husband).
84. Do you believe in fate?
85. Do you think God controls your fate?

References

Ahmad, Zehrunnessa A. and Zeidenstein, Sondra A. 1982. *Rural Women of Bangladesh: Prospects for Change*. Oxford: Pergamon Press.

Agnihotri Gupta, Jyotsna. 1996. *New Freedoms, New Dependencies: New Reproductive Technologies, Women's Health and Autonomy*. Leyden: Universitair Grafisch Bedriff, University of Leyden.

Amjad, Rashid. 1990. 'Urban Planning and Employment Generation in the Asian Megalopolis'. In *Employment Situation*, a monograph published by the International Labor Organization, pp. 123-140. IIS, 1991. 3720–M132. Geneva: International Labor Organization.

Anand, Anita. 1984. 'Rethinking Women and Development'. In *Women in Development*, ISIS Women's International Information and Communication Service. Pennsylvania: New Society.

Ananda Bazar Patrika. 1991. 'Tobu Ey Shahar Agotir Goti'. Editorial, June 25:2. Calcutta: Ananda Bazar Publications.

Anker, Richard. 1982. 'Demographic Change and the Role of Women: A Research Programme in Developing Countries'. In *Women's Roles and Population Trends in the Third World*. Richard Anker, Mayra Buvinic and Nadia Youssef, eds. London: Croom Helm.

———., Mayra Buvinic and Nadia Youssef, eds. 1982. *Women's Roles and Population Trends in the Third World*. London: Croom Helm.

Aslam, Abid. 1992. 'India to Improve Sterilization Programme'. *Population* 18(1):2. January. United Nations Population Fund.

Babb, Florence E. 1990. Review article in *Latin American Research Review* 25(2):236–47.

Banerjee, D. 1971. *Family Planning in India: A Critique and a Perspective*. Delhi: People's Publishing House.

Banerjee, Diptesh. 1984. 'West Bengal: Detours of Stagnation.' *Economic and Political Weekly*. 21(19):975–6.

Banerjee, Nirmala. 1985. *Women Workers in the Unorganized Sector: the Calcutta experience.* Hyderabad: Sangam.

Barnett, Barbara, and Jane Stein. 1998. *Women's Voices, Women's Lives: The Impact of Family Planning*. Women's Studies Project, North Carolina.

Basu, Alaka M. 1984. 'Ignorance of Family Planning Methods in India: An Important Constraint on Use.' *Studies in Family Planning*. 15(3):136–142.

———. 1985. 'Family Planning and the Emergency: An Unanticipated Consequence.' *Economic and Political Weekly* 20(10): 422–5.

———. 1992. *Culture, the Status of Women and Demographic Behaviour*. Oxford: Clarendon Press.

———., and Ramamani Sundar. 1988. 'Domestic Servant as Family Planning Innovator: An Indian Case Study.' *Studies in Family Planning* 19(5):292–8.

Baud, Isa. 1992. *Forms of Production and Women's Labor: Gender Aspects of Industrialization in India and Mexico*. Livelihood and Environment Vol. 1. New Delhi: Sage.

Beneria, Lourdes, and Gita Sen. 1981. 'Accumulation, Reproduction and Women's Role in Economic Development: Boserup Revisited'. *Signs* 7(2):279–8.

———. 1982. 'Class and Gender Inequalities and Women's Role in Economic Development: Theoretical and Practical Implications'. *Feminist Studies* 8(1).

Beneria, Lourdes, and Martha Roldan. 1987. *The Crossroads of Class and Gender: Industrial Homework, Subcontracting, and Household Dynamics in Mexico City*. Chicago: University of Chicago Press.

Bhatt, Ela. 1987. 'The Invisibility of Home-Based Work: The Case of Piece Rate Workers in India.' In *Invisible Hands Women in Home-based Production*. Women and the Household in Asia Vol. 1, ed. Andrea Menefee Singh and Kelles-Viitanen. New Delhi: Sage.

Bhimal, Shefali, and Sunil Jain. 1992. 'In Deeper Trouble'. *India Today*. North American Special Edition. November 30:90–2.

Birdsall, Nancy. 1976. 'Women and Population Studies'. *Signs* 1(3):699–712.

Blanc, Ann K., and Naomi Rutenberg. 1991. 'Coitus and Contraception: The Utility of Data on Sexual Intercourse for Family Planning Programs'. *Studies in Family Planning* 22(3): 162–76.

Borooah, Romy, Barbara A. Yates and Jean Treloggen Peterson. 1985. *Women and Development: An Interdisciplinary Seminar*. Curriculum Guide No.7. Urbana: Office of Women in International Development, University of Illinois at Urbana-Champaign.

Boserup, Ester. 1970. *Women: The Fifth World.* New York: Foreign Policy Association.

Cain, Mead. 1981. 'Risk and Insurance: Perspectives on Fertility and Agrarian Change in India and Bangladesh'. *Population and Development Review* 7:435–74.

CMDA[Calcutta Metropolitan Development Authority]. 1981. 'Project Report for Improved Facilities of Left out Bustee Pockets.' Book No.1/2. Calcutta: M.I. & M.A.D. Sector Planning Wing.

Caldwell, John, P.H. Reddy and Pat Caldwell. 1988. *The Causes of Demographic Change: Experimental Research in South India.* Madison: University of Wisconsin Press.

Campbell, Donald T. 1984. 'Foreword'. In *Case Study Research: Design and Methods*, by Robert K. Yin. Beverley Hills: Sage.

Carroll, Theodora Foster. 1983. *Women and Religious Development in the Third World.* New York: Praeger.

Chanana, Karuna. 1989. 'Introduction'. In *Gender and the Household Domain: Social and Cultural Dimensions*, ed. Maithreyi Krishnaraj and Karuna Chanana.. Vol. 4 of *Women and the Household in Asia*. New Delhi: Sage.

Chatterjee, Biswajeet. 1998. 'Poverty in West Bengal: What Have We Learnt?' *Economic and Political Weekly* 33(47–48):3003–14.

Chatterjee, Meera. 1989. 'Competence and Care for Women: Health Policy Perspectives in the Household Context'. In *Gender and the Household Domain: Social and Cultural Dimensions.* ed. Maithreyi Krishnaraj and Karuna Chanana.. Vol. 4 of *Women and the Household in Asia*. New Delhi: Sage.

Chaudhury, Mahinder. 1989. 'Population Policy in India'. *Population and Environment* 11:101–21.

———. 1990. 'Role of the Social and Cultural Factors in Human Fertility in India.' *Population and Environment* 12(2):117–37.

Chilman, Catherine. 1973. 'Some Psychological Aspects of Fertility, Family Planning and Population Policy in the US'. In *Psychological Perspectives on Population* ed. James T. Fawcett. New York: Basic Books. pp. 163–84.

Collins, Randall and Scott Coltrane. 1991. *Sociology of Marriage and the Family: Gender, Love and Property.* Chicago: Nelson-Hall Publishers.

Cvetkovich, G.T. and W.J. Lonner. 1973. 'A Transnational Comparison of Individual Birth Planning Decisions for Hypothetical families'. *Journal of Cross-Cultural Psychology* 4: 470–80.

Das, Veena. 1985. 'The Body as Metaphor: Socialization of Women in Punjabi Urban Families'. *Manushi* 25:2-6.

Dasgupta, Biplab, Mohit Bhattacharya, Dev Kumar Basu, Monidip Chatterjee and Tapan K. Banerjee. 1991. *Calcutta's Urban Future: Agonies from the Past and Prospects for the Future.* Calcutta: Government of West Bengal.

Dasgupta, Monika, Lincoln C. Chen and T.N. Krishnan. 1995. *Women's Health in India: Risk and Vulnerability*. Oxford: Oxford University Press.

Dasgupta, Swapan. 1992. 'Twain Cannot Meet'. *Sunday* May 31-Jun. 6. Calcutta: Anandabazar Publications.

Datta, Anuradha. 1984. 'Working Population in Calcutta Metropolitan District: A Critique of Sectoral Classification'. *Economic and Political Weekly.* 19(29):1166–8.

Demerath, Nicholas J. 1976. *Birth Control and Foreign Policy: The Alternative to Family Planning*. New York: Harper and Row.

Desai, Neera, and Krishnaraj, Maithreyi. 1987. *Women and Society in India.* Delhi: Ajanta.

Desai, Neera, and Vibhuti Patel. eds. 1989. *Critical Review of Researches in Women's Studies 1975-1988.* Bombay: SNDT Women's University, Research Centre for Women's Studies.

Desai, A.R. 1980. *Urban Family and Family Planning in India.* Bombay: Popular Prakashan.

Dharmalingam, A., and S. Philip Morgan. 1996. 'Women's Work, Autonomy, and Birth Control: Evidence from Two South Indian Villages'. *UN Population Studies* 50(Jul.):2, 187–201.

Dixon-Mueller, Ruth. 1996. 'The Seuality Connection in Reproductive Health'. In *Studies in Family Planning* 2(5):269–82. Originally published by the Population Council.

Dubey, D.C. and A. Bardhan. 1975. 'Mass Acceptance of Vasectomy: The Role of Social Interaction and Incentives in Social Change'. In *Population and Social Organization, ed.* Moni Nag. Chicago: Aldine.

Dutt, Devina, Nabanita Dutt, Gauri Lankesh and Minu Jain. 1992. 'Not My Problem! Examining the Male Attitude to Contraception'. *Sunday* 19-25 Jan.: 78–81. Calcutta: Anandabazar.

Dyson, Tim, and Mick Moore. 1983. 'On Kinship Structure, Female Autonomy and Demographic Behavior in India.' *Population and Development Review* 9:61–76.

Dyson, Tim, and Nigel Crook, eds. 1984. *India's Demography*. New Delhi: South Asian Publishers.

England, Paula and George Farkas. 1986. *Household, Employment and Gender: A Social Economic and Demographic View*. New York: Aldine De Gruyter.

General Social Surveys, 1972–1991: *Cumulative Code Book*. 1991. Conducted for the National Data Program for the Social Sciences, at National Opinion Research Center, University of Chicago. Data Distributed by the Roper Center for Public Opinion Research, University of Connecticut.

Government of India. 1981. *Report of the Census of India*. New Delhi: Indian Census Bureau.

———. 1990. 'Estimated age-specific fertility rates and other fertility indicators, India, 1987'. *Sample Registration Bulletin*, December. New Delhi: Ministry of Home Affairs.

———. 1991. *Report of the Census of India*. New Delhi: Indian Census Bureau.

Government of West Bengal. 1986. Bulletin of the Department of Health and Family Welfare. Calcutta: Government of West Bengal.

Groat, H. T., and A.G. Neal. 1967. *'Social Psychological Correlates of Urban Fertility'*. *American Sociological Review*. 32:945–59.

Guha Thakurta, Poronjoy. 1991. 'Hitting Rock Bottom: Hard Decisions Needed to Face the Worst Fiscal Crisis'. *India Today*. North American Special Edition 16(1):49–50.

Health on the March. 1996–97. Calcutta: State Bureau of Health Intelligence, Directorate of Health Services, West Bengal.

Joseph, Ammu. 1992. 'India's Population 'Bomb' Explodes over Women'. *Ms* November/Devember 3(3):12–14.

Kabeer, Naila. 1985. 'Do Women Really Gain from High Fertility?' In *Women, Work and Ideology in the Third World*, ed. Haleh Afshar. New York: Tavistock. pp. 83–108,

Kandiyoti, Denis. 1989. Review article in *Signs* 14:939–42.

Kakar, Sudhir. 1990. *Intimate Relations: Exploring Indian Sexuality*. Chicago: University of Chicago Press.

Lebra, Joyce, Joy Paulson and Jana Everett, eds. 1984. *Women and Work in India: Continuity and Change*. New Delhi: Promilla Publishers.

Mamdani, Mahmud. 1973. *The Myth of Population Control: Family, Caste and Class in an Indian Village.* New York: Monthly Review Press.

Mandelbaum, David. 1974. *Human Fertility in India: Social Components and Policy Perspectives.* Berkeley: University of California Press.

Mathew, P.M.. 1992. 'Women's Industrial Employment in India.' In *Class, State and Development in India,* ed. Berch Berberoglu,. New Delhi: Sage.

Mazumdar, Vina, and Kumud Sharma. 1990. 'Sexual Division of Labor and the Subordination of Women: A Reappraisal from India'. In *Persistent Inequalities,* ed. Irene Tinker. New York: Oxford University Press.

Mencher, Joan P. 1989. 'Women Agricultural Laborers and Land Owners in Kerala and Tamil Nadu: Some Questions about Gender Autonomy in the Household'. In *Gender and the Household Domain: Social and Cultural Dimensions,* ed. Maithreyi Krishnaraj and Karuna Chanana. Vol. 4 of *Women and the Household in Asia.* New Delhi: Sage.

Michaelson, Karen. L. 1981. 'Population Policy, Family Size and the Reproduction of the Labor Force in India: The Case of Bombay'. In *And the Poor Get Children: Radical Perspectives on Population Dynamics,* ed. Karen L. Michaelson. New York: Monthly Review Press.

Minault, Gail. 1986. 'Women in Contemporary India: The Quest for Equal Participation and Justice'. In *India 2000: The Next Fifteen Years,* ed. James R. Poach. New Delhi: Allied Publishers.

Morakvasic, Mirjana. 1981. 'Sexuality and the Control of Procreation'. In *Of Marriage and the Market: Woman's Subordination in International Perspective,* ed. Kate Young, Carol Wolkowitz and Roslyn McCullagh. London: CSE Books. pp. 127–44.

Mukhopadhyay, Swapna, and R. Savithri. 1998. *Poverty, Gender and Reproductive Choice: An Analysis of Linkages.* New Delhi: Manohar.

Myrdal, Jan. 1986. *India Waits.* Chicago: Lake View Press.

Nag, Moni. 1972. 'Sex, Culture and Human Fertility: India and the United States.' *Current Anthropology.* 13(2):231-237.

———. 1996. *Sexual Behaviour and Aids in India.* New Delhi: Vikas.

Nagchowdhury, Subrata. 1991. 'Where Money for Projects Goes Down the Drain'. *The Statesman* Mar. 28. Calcutta: Statesman House.

Nair, Hema. 1992. 'South Asian Films by Women: Making It Personal'. *Ms* November/December 3(3):68–9.

Nandy, Ashish. 1980. *At the Edge of Psychology: Essays in Politics and Culture.* New Delhi: Oxford University Press.

Narayana, G. and John F. Kantner. 1992. *Doing the Needful: The Dilemma of India's Population Policy.* Boulder: Westview Press.

National Longitudinal Study of Youth (NLSY). 1992. Columbus: Ohio State University, Center for Human Resource Research.

Omvedt, Gail. 1992. 'Capitalist Agriculture and Rural Classes in India'. In *Class, State and Development in India,* ed. Berch Berberoglu. New Delhi: Sage.

Pakrasi, K. and C. Malakar. 1967. 'The Relationship Between Family Type and Fertility'. *Milbank Memorial Fund Quarterly.* 45:451–60.

Papanek, Hanna. 1990. 'To Each Less Than She Needs, From Each More Than She Can Do'. In *Persistent Inequalities,* ed. Irene Tinker. New York and Oxford: Oxford University Press.

Parpart, Jane. 1989. *Women and Development in Africa: Comparative Perspectives.* Lannam: University Press of America.

Patel, Tulsi. 1990. 'The Sterilization Decision and Family Structure: Case Study of an Indian Village'. *Indian Journal of Sociology.* December: 23-35.

Poffenberger, Thomas and Shirley B. Poffenberger. 1973. 'The Social Psychology of Fertility in India in a Village in India'. In *Psychological Perspectives on Population,* ed. James T. Fawcett. New York: Basic Books.

Pollack, Scarlett. 1985. 'Sex and the Contraceptive Act'. In *The Sexual Politics of Reproduction,* ed. Hillary Homans. Vermont: Gower.

Prakash, Padma. 1991. 'Identifying Health Needs of Women'. *The Hindu Magazine.* October 27:1.

Qadeer, Imrana. 1998. 'Reproductive Health: A Public Health Perspective'. *Economic and Political Weekly* 33(41)2675–84.

Rainwater, Lee. 1960. *And the Poor Get Children.* Chicago: Quadrangle Books.

Ramu, G.N. 1988. *Family Structure and Fertility: Emerging Patterns in an Indian City.* New Delhi: Sage Publications.

Rathgeber, Eva M. 1990. 'WID, WAD, GAD: Trends in Research and Practice'. (Participation of Women in Development Processes). *The Journal of Developing Areas.* 24:489–502.

Roberts, Bryan. 1989. Review article. In *Economic Development and Cultural Change* 37:447–9.

Roberts, H. 1981. 'Male Hegemony in Family Planning'. In *Women, Health and Reproduction*, ed. H. Roberts. London: Routledge and Kegan Paul. pp. 1–17.

Roldan, Martha. 1988. 'Renegotiating the Marital Contract: Intra-household Patterns of Money Allocation and Women's sobordination Among Domestic Outworkers in Mexico City,' in *A Home Divided: Women and Income in the Third World*. Daisy Dwyer and Judith Bruce, eds. Callifornia: Stanford University Press.

Sandhu, Jameet. 1996. *Sociology of Fertility*. New Delhi: Rawat.

Safilios-Rothschild, Constantina. 1982. 'Female Power, Autonomy and Demographic Change in the Third World'. In *Women's Roles and Population Trends in the Third World*, ed. Richard Anker, Mayra Buvinic and Nadia Youssef. London: Croom Helm.

Sen, Amartya K. 1995. 'Gender Inequality and Theories of Justice'. In *Women, Culture and Development: A Study of Human Capabilities*, ed. Martha Nussbaum and Jonathan Cover. Oxford: Clarendon Press.

Sen, Gita and Caren Grown. 1987. *Development, Crises and Alternative Visions Third World Women's Perspectives*. New York: Monthly Review Press.

Singh, Andrea Menefee. 1984. 'Rural-to Urban Migration of Women in India: Patterns and Implications'. In *Women in the Cities of Asia*, ed. James T. Fawcett, Khoo Shew-Ean and Peter C.Smith. Boulder: Westview Press.

Som. Nisit. 1987. 'Bustees, Pavement Dwellers and Refugees of Calcutta'. In *The Urban Experience Calcutta: Essays in Honor of Professor Nisith R. Ray*, ed. Pradip Sinha. Calcutta: Riddhi-India.

Srinivasan, K., Shireen J. Jejeebhoy, Richard A. Easterlin and Eileen M. Crimmins. 1984. 'Factors Affecting Fertility Control in India: A Cross-Sectional Study'. *Population and Development Review*. 10:273–96.

Standing, Hilary. 1985. 'Resources, Wages, and Power: the Impact of Women's Employment on the Urban Bengali Household'. In *Women, Work and Ideology in the Third World*, ed. Haleh Afshar. New York: Tavistock. pp 232-255.

Tinker, Irene, ed. 1990. 'The Making of a Field: Advocates, Practitioners and Scholars'. In *Persistent Inequalities*, ed. Irene Tinker. Oxford: Oxford University Press.

Vijayan, Aleyamma. 1990. 'Struggling with Hope-The Story of Women Fish Vendors of South Kerala'. *Manushi* 61:9–11.

Vock, Jane. 1988. 'Demographic Theories and Women's Reproductive Labor'. In *Patriarchy and Class: African Women in the Home and the Workforce*, ed. Sharon B. Stichter and Jane L. Parpart. Boulder: Westview Press.

Wadley, Susan. 1977. 'Women and the Hindu Tradition'. *Signs*. 3:113–25.

Yin, Robert K. 1984. *Case Study Research: Design and Methods.* Volume 5 of *Applied Social Science Methods*. Beverly Hills: Sage.

Young, Kate, ed. 1988. *Women and Economic Development: Local, Regional and National Planning Strategies.* New York: UNESCO.

INDEX